POLICE
UNDER
PRESSURE

D1477573

Recent Titles in
Contributions in Criminology and Penology

Chinese Subculture and Criminality: Non-traditional Crime Groups in America
Ko-lin Chin

A Sword for the Convicted: Representing Indigent Defendants on Appeal
David T. Wasserman

Delinquency in Puerto Rico: The 1970 Birth Cohort Study
Dora Nevares, Marvin E. Wolfgang, and Paul E. Tracy with the Collaboration of Steven Aurand

Waging the Battle Against Drunk Driving: Issues, Countermeasures, and Effectiveness
Gerald D. Robin

Policing Western Europe: Politics, Professionalism, and Public Order, 1850–1940
Clive Emsley and Barbara Weinberger, editors

Policing a Socialist Society: The German Democratic Republic
Nancy Travis Wolfe

Domestic Marijuana: A Neglected Industry
Ralph A. Weisheit

Personality and Peer Influence in Juvenile Corrections
Martin Gold and D. Wayne Osgood

Bad Guys and Good Guys: Moral Polarization and Crime
Daniel S. Claster

Innovative Strategies in the Treatment of Drug Abuse
James A. Inciardi, Frank M. Tims, and Bennett W. Fletcher, editors

Coca and Cocaine: An Andean Perspective
Felipe E. Mac Gregor, editor

POLICE UNDER PRESSURE

Resolving Disputes

ROBERT COULSON

HV
7936
.P47
C68
1993,
West

Contributions in Criminology and Penology,
Number 40

GREENWOOD PRESS
Westport, Connecticut • London

Library of Congress Cataloging-in-Publication Data

Coulson, Robert.
    Police under pressure : resolving disputes / Robert Coulson.
        p. cm.—(Contributions in criminology and penology, ISSN
0732–4464 ; no. 40)
    Includes bibliographical references and index.
    ISBN 0–313–28791–0 (alk. paper)
    1. Police—United States—Personnel management. 2. Collective
bargaining—Police—United States. 3. Arbitration, Industrial—
United States. 4. Police—United States—Job stress. I. Title.
II. Series.
HV7936.P47C68   1993
350.74′068′3—dc20   92–35551

British Library Cataloguing in Publication Data is available.

Copyright © 1993 by Robert Coulson

All rights reserved. No portion of this book may be
reproduced, by any process or technique, without the
express written consent of the publisher.

Library of Congress Catalog Card Number: 92–35551
ISBN: 0–313–28791–0
ISSN: 0732–4464

First published in 1993

Greenwood Press, 88 Post Road West, Westport, CT 06881
An imprint of Greenwood Publishing Group, Inc.

Printed in the United States of America

The paper used in this book complies with the
Permanent Paper Standard issued by the National
Information Standards Organization (Z39.48–1984).

10 9 8 7 6 5 4 3 2 1

Contents

POLICE
UNDER
PRESSURE

Introduction

This book is about police officers, the departments that employ them, and the labor disputes between them. Based on the recent awards of labor arbitrators, this book raises tough questions about how police officers are treated and about how they are being used. This book takes the view that police management needs to be updated and that the police mission has gone askew. Rather than encouraging officers to carry out their traditional function of keeping the peace, police management is trying to stop the sale of drugs, a struggle that pits police officers against major segments of the urban community.

Police officers say that they are caught between their difficult, hazardous work and a hostile community, and this book supports that assertion. It also tells what it is like to be a cop in modern America.

The Rodney King incident in Los Angeles raised many important questions, such as:

- What motivated police officers to engage in such violence against a black suspect?

- Was the beating of Rodney King symptomatic of an attitude that some police officers have toward minority males?

- Have the police become alienated from the communities they serve?

The riots that followed the Rodney King verdict show how much anger and social chaos is lurking under the surface of urban America. The police provide a primary layer of protection from the horror of unrestrained vandalism and violence. Can we afford to be without strong, effective police protection?

Police officers are recruited when they are young, usually in their early twenties. Their physical condition is tested, then they are given training, but perhaps this is not enough. Because the responsibilities of police officers are demanding and they are expected to deal with every kind of urban problem, they can never have enough training. After a recruit is assigned to a precinct, the real job begins because they then discover that much of their work requires them to resolve complex and emotional problems.

Many of the incidents described in this book involve conflicts that require a mature understanding of human nature and the use of sophisticated judgment. These cases are not fictitious. The police officers involved were disciplined and felt that their treatment was unfair; therefore, they requested that their union file an arbitration, believing that only an impartial arbitrator could correct the injustice. This does not mean that police departments are generally unfair, but like many other authoritarian organizations, they sometimes are insensitive in their treatment of employees.

Labor arbitrators bring a unique outlook to their cases, and awards are based on the arbitrator's extensive experience with employees and employers. Each award deals with the facts of the case being decided and reflects the employment policies of the particular police department. Each grievance is symptomatic of the working environment of the police officer involved.

The cases discussed in this book raise some interesting questions, such as:

- What do these labor awards indicate about the working life of police officers?
- How could each of the disputes have been avoided?
- Should higher standards be imposed upon police officers than on other workers?
- Should a police officer be disciplined for breaking the law? Should there be a more flexible standard when an officer is off-duty?
- How should a cop who misbehaves be punished?

Job security is particularly important to public employees, such as police officers, because many of them expect to work for one community during their entire career. Civil service laws protect most public employees against being fired unjustly. Police officers usually have the right to an administrative review when they are terminated, in addition to their rights as union members to submit unjust discharge issues to labor arbitration.

Many police departments have been unionized. Although there is no single, national police union, as is the case in some job classifications, many police unions exist, and some are affiliated with large labor organizations. Police officers who are members of a union are protected by a collective bargaining contract that protects their working rights. The grievance procedure gives union members the right to file a grievance when they think that the contract has been violated, and management must respond to the grievance. If the union and the employer cannot resolve the grievance, the issues can be submitted to an impartial expert on such matters, an arbitrator.

On behalf of its members, the union can demand that contractual issues be submitted to an arbitrator. After hearing the case, the arbitrator issues an award, with a written opinion explaining the reasons for the decision that is final and binding. The Labor Arbitration Rules of the American Arbitration Association (AAA) are printed at the end of this book. They are a model for grievance arbitration procedures throughout the United States.

Grievances usually arise after some disciplinary action has been taken by an employer. Most grievances are settled informally between representatives of the union and the employer. Only the more intractable grievances must be arbitrated. As you read the cases in this book, you may wonder why some of them needed to be arbitrated because some of the issues may seem trivial. Why were the parties unable to resolve them?

In this book, arbitrators are identified. Many are well known, have decided thousands of labor cases, and are experts in the field of labor relations. Through such experienced and sharp eyes, the view of the issues is brought into focus. Sometimes, you may conclude that a particular arbitrator's judgment does not coincide with your own. As with most human systems, there is room for error; even arbitrators make mistakes.

It is not always easy for an arbitrator to obtain a comprehensive understanding of the relevant facts, particularly when an incident occurred many months before the hearing. An arbitrator must rely on the testimony presented at the hearing, which can be unreliable. Witnesses may have been subjected to intense pressure, and personal loyalties or career considerations may color the testimony, particularly when organizational pressure has been applied to the witness. When someone is afraid to tell the truth, an arbitrator may never discover what really happened.

Disagreements over salaries also arise. These are called "interest" disputes and are usually resolved through collective bargaining between the union and the municipality. Police officers are usually compensated on the basis of rank and seniority, with periodic increases within some established range. During each bargaining cycle, the union tries to increase those salary ranges whereas the employer is concerned about how police salaries relate to those of other municipal workers. Nonwage demands also may impact on other city employees. Some of the cases in this book show how complicated such bargaining can become and raise difficult concerns about municipal employment relations.

The collective bargaining contract between the police union and the local government establishes many of the conditions under which police officers work. An arbitrator is bound by the contract. A court will defer to an arbitrator's decision, but only if it is grounded on contract language. An arbitrator is not authorized to modify the contract or to decide that a particular provision is undesirable but must apply the language as written, because the contract itself is the final authority. Only when the contract is ambiguous may an arbitrator interpret the language.

Grievance arbitration is an extension of collective bargaining where a victory by either party in arbitration can be negotiated away or recaptured at the bargaining table. The relationship is always subject to change but during the term of the contract the rights and obligations of the parties are fixed.

The cases in this book have been selected from hundreds of recent arbitration awards. Many appeared in the AAA's monthly publication, "Labor Arbitration in Government." Others were culled from similar published reports. They have been chosen because they illustrate some of the stressful situations that police officers encounter on the job.

Put yourself in the place of the arbitrator. Did the arbitrator make the correct decision? How would you have decided the case? One of the purposes of this book is to demonstrate that arbitrators generally reach rational conclusions. Also, the intention is to raise fundamental questions about the police function. What should be the role of the police? Is their proper task to keep the peace? Should they primarily be used to respond to emergency calls? What kind of law enforcement actually reduces crime? What priority should be given to apprehending drug dealers? What impact does such work have on other parts of the justice system?

This book benefited from the research of Mark Shelton, during his summer internship with the AAA, while a student at the Cornell School of Industrial and Labor Relations. He surveyed the literature of police arbitration and helped select and summarize the case reports.

I would also like to thank Darrel W. Stephens, Executive Director of the Police Executive Research Forum and labor arbitrator Charlotte Gold for their helpful comments about an early draft of this book.

CHAPTER 1

The Autocratic Nature of Police Departments

Even though the rights of police officers are spelled out in collective bargaining contracts, individual cops are on dangerous ground when they challenge departmental policy. Those confrontations pit the individual officer against the department and against a structure of supervision and management that is notoriously authoritarian.

In most grievance arbitration cases, the relationship between the officer and supervision has deteriorated. Compromise is no longer possible, and the grievance cannot be settled through negotiations. When an arbitrator is called in, these kinds of situations are usually beyond the point of compromise.

"Conduct unbecoming an officer" is a frequent charge in police disciplinary proceedings, and the phrase appears in many collective bargaining contracts. It is a broad definition that is applied to insubordination, as well as to general misbehavior. Insubordination is particularly threatening to authoritarian organizations like police departments.

Police departments adopt elaborate rules of behavior. Some are imposed by state regulation, some reflect the views of a police commissioner, and others have been accumulated from decades of organizational experience. Codes of behavior are also sometimes negotiated as part of the collective bargaining process.

In the police environment, behavioral regulations take on great importance, because an authoritarian command structure usually emphasizes the importance of such rules. Although many police administrators pursue an academic education, most started as cops, and much of what they learn about management is learned on the job. Police administrators must operate in a complex environment where they deal with politicians, other municipal departments, labor unions, the public, and the press. Like other managers, they must follow organizational policies, and they often make decisions under pressure. It should not be surprising that sometimes they forget to consider their employees.

Middle level police administrators may have limited authority. They may act in a certain way for political reasons, because they may be required to do so by state or federal laws, or because they may have to operate on a tight leash. Their policies may have been determined for them by the commissioner—without their input—which means that they find themselves defending actions initiated higher up in their department.

Emergencies add another unpredictable element to an already difficult relationship. Hostile publicity, unexpected emergencies, charges of corruption, and fiscal shortfalls may influence departmental actions. The individual cop is given orders and must comply.

Police officers often work under stress, particularly in communities that are trying to stamp out the distribution of illegal drugs. In some neighborhoods, the police are literally at war, and violence and the threat of injury are part of their daily work. While reading the cases that follow, think about those aspects of police work in the particular community where the incident arose: the discipline, the danger, and the quality of the employment relationship.

Many private employers have concluded that it is efficient to manage employees by giving them a sense of ownership and encouraging them to set their own goals and to exercise initiative. Motivational techniques are used to reinforce that approach, including objective performance reviews, bonuses, and equity participation. Those management techniques are seldom emphasized by police departments, which are more likely to depend on tight supervision, work rules, and quotas. The operations of many police departments are based on command and control—the precinct captain gives the orders, and supervision sees that they are carried out.

Command and control management theories have been abandoned by many employers, but seldom are they abandoned by the police. Perhaps it is time to mix a little green in with the blue. When patrolmen are treated like cogs, they tend to adopt a low risk, robotic approach to their job. They follow orders and become less willing to exercise initiative or to initiate community activity.

Some police departments become captivated by trivia. There are disputes over the design of uniforms, shoe polish, and name tags, and rules as to hair cuts and beards create seemingly unnecessary squabbles. A police officer may regard such rules as irrelevant and demeaning, particularly after a difficult day when his or her life may have been in jeopardy.

THE NATURE OF POLICE GRIEVANCES

An early study by Helen Lavan and Cameron Carley, when they were on the faculty at DePaul University, covered sixty-four grievance arbitrations involving police officers. They identified some unique aspects of police grievances and broke new ground in the field. They found that police officers won a higher percentage of cases than grievants in other kinds of employment, particularly when a public complaint triggered the disciplinary action. In their sample, 76.6 percent of the cases were won by the union, and grievants were often supported by their own supervisors, something seldom encountered in other areas of employment in labor arbitration. A public complaint was initiated in 19 percent of the sample cases in the DePaul study, and usually the officer's supervisors supported the behavior.

These cases arose in the early days of police unionization. In about one-third of the cases studied, the arbitrator ordered the police department to make changes in its disciplinary practices. Now police departments have become more sophisticated, and a contemporary study would probably indicate less need to amend such procedures.

Certain kinds of issues are commonly arbitrated, such as the just cause of disciplinary actions and interpretation of contract language. The DePaul study recommended, as to discipline cases, that the contract carefully define the duties and obligations of police officers, both on- and off-duty. Collective bargaining contracts, therefore, have become increasingly specific.

The study also pointed out that other tribunals are available to resolve complaints against police officers. Criminal courts, departmental boards, and city councils provide jurisdiction over citizen complaints and disciplinary investigations. Although labor arbitration is not the exclusive remedy, it has become increasingly popular.

Collective bargaining by police officers has a stormy history. The police were viewed as natural strike breakers. How could police officers be allowed to form a union? Since those early days, many states have authorized police unions, but others do not have such enabling laws, and a few refuse to recognize police unions.

With or without such laws, the police in most major cities have organized—partially to improve their wages and partially to obtain job security. Unionization has raised police salaries and improved their fringe benefits, and it has made it difficult to fire a police officer without good cause.

THE IMPACT OF COLLECTIVE BARGAINING

Collective bargaining between a police department and a union may reflect the hostility that authoritarian relationships often induce. Union officials bring to the bargaining table the multiple demands of their members, and the lack of job participation in management that exists in many departments becomes part of the baggage that antagonizes contract negotiations.

A quasimilitary atmosphere may also color police organizations. In *Police Personnel Administration*, W. J. Bopp points out that "the American police are generally organized in a semi-military manner, a heritage that dates back centuries. Today this philosophy is as strongly entrenched as it ever was." This was in 1974.

The bargaining atmosphere between an employer and a union depends on the relationship between individual employees and their supervisors. The authoritarian nature of police organizations permeates what is expressed in collective negotiations across the bargaining table. In any case, employment relations in the public sector operate in a unique environment. Civil service laws protect most public employees, but, in the case of police officers, this is subject to an expectation that police owe an unusually high standard of performance to their community and to their local government, creating obligations as to public safety and morality above the level imposed on other public employees.

POLICE OFFICERS ARE SUBJECT TO HIGHER STANDARDS

Cops are held to high standards by their supervisors, but not every police officer can meet that ideal standard. Sometimes, officers succumb to temptation and violate the law. In other jobs, employees are often allowed to continue working after breaking a law. Cops, however, are different, because law enforcement is the police officer's job. How can a police officer be expected to uphold the law that the officer has broken?

Most people would agree that an officer who breaks the law should be punished. But what if the officer is acquitted? That question arose in a case involving a police officer from Haverhill, Massachusetts, who was charged with conspiring with a convicted drug dealer. He was acquitted, but later filed a grievance against the City asking to be compensated for his legal fees.

The grievant had been accused of exchanging confidential law enforcement information in return for cocaine. He was tried but found not guilty. Afterwards, the officer asserted that his legal expenses, amounting to $108,000, should be paid by the City.

The grievant had been a detective and his father was chief of police in Haverhill. The case involved the officer's relationship with a major drug dealer, whom he said that he had met at a health club soon after becoming a police officer in 1986. The drug dealer had asked the grievant for information on certain license plates so that he could identify the vehicles' owners. The dealer had been worried about being investigated by the state police and wanted to identify the people who were tailing him.

The grievant provided the drug dealer with the information but testified later that he was just trying to lead him on. He claimed that a state police officer had asked him to investigate the dealer but said he could not recall the officer's name. There was no record of any such request.

The investigation was prompted by a search of the drug dealer's home, during which a ledger was discovered listing, among other transactions, cocaine sales to the grievant. The Drug Enforcement Agency placed a wiretap on the grievant's phone and intercepted conversations that suggested that he was dealing in cocaine.

At the grievant's trial, his father testified that the grievant had tested positive for cocaine. It was also revealed that he had been hospitalized for drug addiction and placed on administrative leave during the summer of 1987.

At the arbitration hearing, the union argued that the City should pay the grievant's legal expenses. The union argued that to limit the City's responsibility for such fees to cases involving assault, use of excessive force, or civil rights violations would ignore the reality of police work. It argued that a police officer is involved in such varied situations that it is almost impossible to limit the coverage; and the City owed the officer reimbursement for his legal fees.

The City, on the other hand, said that the criminal charges were not based on activities occurring while the officer was on-duty and that in order to be covered an officer must be on-duty. The City argued that the grievant had been engaged in his own affairs, and the indictment was the result of a police investigation, not a complaint from the public.

Arbitrator Tim Bornstein, a Harvard Law School graduate, looked at the language of the contract, particularly the phrase requiring that "the events surrounding the complaint happen while the officer was on duty." In his decision, Bornstein pointed out that there was no support for the grievant's claim that he was investigating the drug dealer. To the contrary, there was plenty of evidence showing that the grievant was a customer with a personal relationship with the dealer. In denying the grievance, Bornstein said that the grievant's assertion that the case involved police work or that the grievant was on-duty could "hardly be taken seriously."

PROPER POLICE FUNCTION

Some people believe that police departments should give more priority to serving the community and providing social services. Former New York Police Commissioner Lee P. Brown tried to turn the New York City Police Department in that direction. His plan required an entire shift in values that started at the top. The New York Police Department would have to take responsibility for social conditions in the neighborhoods—an awesome task.

The traditional model of police work has emphasized responding to radio calls. Community policing requires a different approach, that is, a partnership between the people in the neighborhoods and the police officers. Commissioner Brown was trying to install this change in New York City, where the department has over 27,000 uniformed and 10,000 nonuniformed personnel. According to Brown, "The command and control culture of the police department doesn't treat officers as intelligent, creative and trustworthy people." If he is correct, the attitudes of thousands of superior officers will have to undergo a radical change.

The problems in high crime areas may well result from a failure to provide adequate social services. Poor education and broken families produce young people who are unable to obtain or to hold jobs and who are alienated from society. They are tinder waiting to explode.

In the United States, the criminal justice system is supposed to enforce the law. Police officers arrest criminals when they violate the law, but in doing this they apprehend thousands of young men and send them into the criminal courts. In New York City alone, over 300,000 people were arrested in 1991, mostly young, unemployed males. All across the country, thousands of young men are incarcerated, even though most authorities say that crime will increase so long as no serious effort is made to address the causes of crime.

Americans know that the present approach is not working. Fear of crime is a growing concern, but there is little consensus as to what should be done about it. Unlike most developed countries, Americans pretend that all parents can care for their own children and that every kid will grow up healthy, educated, and able to get a job, but this is not true. All too many urban young men are uneducated, unemployed, and involved in illicit activities. The drug scene provides jobs and a life-style that looks better to many of them than having no job. High crime environments such as these put extra pressure on local police.

A realistic approach to reducing crime would be to recognize that drug sales are a well-financed and well-organized business, with deep roots in the community. Police departments may have to adopt a different approach. The emphasis now is on catching drug dealers, and relatively less attention is given to problem solving and working with community groups, but this may have to change. Community organization and problem solving with a broader understanding of social problems must replace the current emphasis on fighting drugs by running around in patrol cars.

Many cities in the United States have large minority populations. Many of these suffer from chronic social problems, and many are poor, relatively uneducated, and unemployed. The white police officer cruising around in a patrol car too often looks like the representative of an occupying power rather than someone who wants to help.

The view from a patrol car in a high crime area is not reassuring either. People look alien, if not sullen, speak a strange dialect, and are capable of sudden violence. Of the over 20,000 homicides in America in 1991, most took place in minority neighborhoods. There is no temptation for a police officer to step out on the sidewalk in such a neighborhood, unless the situation requires some sort of police action. It has become typical, therefore, for patrol cars to drive directly from one assignment to another.

Anyone who watches television becomes aware that police work sometimes involves life-threatening events with cops reacting to criminals. Tense confrontations have become symbolic of American law enforcement, even though the day-to-day work of an average officer is far more mundane. Community work is less exciting but may be more effective in creating peaceful neighborhoods and more productive of positive community attitudes.

Cops are not always convinced that community work is preferable, because responding to emergency calls may appear to be the more important part of their work. Real police work, some of them believe, involves apprehending and arresting law breakers. Anything else is mere social work. Many police officers see their task as fighting crime, not as being primarily in the business of solving social problems. This may be the major problem facing reformers who want the police to play a different role. Police officers must be convinced that maintaining a cohesive society is the most important part of their job. The environment in which cops work may have made many cynical. But different attitudes will be created when community leaders become concerned about their communities and are willing to advocate fundamental changes, such as sending the police off on a new social mission.

Imposing the criminal justice system is not the only way to deal with crime. Many antisocial behaviors do not require a criminal law response but can be treated in other ways, such as through counseling or the social services. The cop can be a problem solver working within the community.

This vision is the essence of community policing, where the police officer works with the people. Using that approach, a police officer becomes a manager and does not simply respond to radio calls or try to arrest as many people as possible, but attempts to understand peoples' concerns, tries to be accessible, and takes responsibility for the community.

As you read the cases in this book, you will recognize situations where police officers have been poorly used, subjected to unnecessary frustrations, and treated almost as children. Would these kinds of grievances have arisen if the officers involved had been working for a police department committed to community policing?

SUMMARY

Police departments are autocratic, top-down organizations. They expect police officers to be exemplary employees, but in the past, they have not trusted them to operate independently.

Modern management techniques have yet to be percolated into this branch of city government. In the cases that follow the effect of this style of management will become clear.

CHAPTER 2

Police Officers Must Make Snap Decisions

Violence and crime are among the most important reasons we must have a police department. When people misbehave, they disrupt society, and the government must protect itself, usually by using the police, the instrument of the state. Sometimes, though, the police may overstep their limits. This chapter deals with such situations where police officers were charged with using excessive force in reacting to crime.

In theory, people who break the law are arrested, then they are taken to a precinct house and booked until court action can be arranged. The police officer who responds to a reported crime is expected to exercise discretion and to react on the spot, often without knowing all the facts.

Decisions frequently have to be made under pressure. An officer may be worried about losing control or may be diverted by what is going on, or the officer's situation may be hazardous. Nevertheless, action must be taken, and any decision made under these conditions may be reviewed by the officer's supervisors, by the public, or perhaps by the press. Police officers work in a fish bowl.

In this chapter, police officers had to justify their behavior before an arbitrator.

A CASE OF DEMOTION FOR EXCESSIVE VIOLENCE

A police sergeant in the city of Claremont in Massachusetts responded with two other officers to a reported fight at the Knights of Columbus Hall, where they found one of the combatants being held down on the ground. When the man refused to calm down, the sergeant had him handcuffed and attempted to put him into a police car. When the prisoner continued to kick and thrash around, the sergeant put leg irons on him and had him carried to the car. Inside, the man attempted to kick the windows. The sergeant then handcuffed the leg irons to the metal grate in the car. Finally, the sergeant "cap stunned" the prisoner with a mace like substance.

After driving the prisoner back to the police station, the sergeant pulled him out of the car, threw him against the wall, and taunted him for not resisting, although the man was still under the influence of the mace. Then, according to the testimony of several officers, the sergeant dragged him into a jail cell where he slammed his head against the cell bunk, kneeled and jumped on his back, ripped his pants, and washed his face with water from the toilet. The other officers reported the sergeant's behavior, and, after an investigation, he was demoted and put on probation.

A full hearing was held after the sergeant's union, American Federation of State, County, and Municipal Employees (AFSCME) Council 93 filed a grievance. The arbitrator, Gary D. Altman, listened to the testimony from the officers who witnessed these events and decided that the City had just cause to penalize the grievant and that the demotion was appropriate. The grievant had used excessive force in violation of the department's rules. However, he concluded that probation, which would subject the grievant to summary dismissal, would violate the agreement.

The arbitrator made a point of the fact that this sergeant was expected to be a leader, and although supervisors should be demoted only in extraordinary situations, the facts of this case indicated that this grievant could no longer effectively perform his responsibilities as a supervisor. Having tried to cover up his actions, he could no longer be trusted.

SHOOTING TO KILL

In a case from Houston, Texas, an experienced white patrol officer was put on indefinite suspension for shooting a 24-year-old black male who had been stopped for an alleged traffic violation, during the administration of Commissioner Lee P. Brown, who was later head of the New York City Police Department.

The incident occurred on Scott Street in Houston on November 15, 1989, and there were several witnesses. Shortly before 1 AM, the grievant was in his police car and saw the suspect driving a 1980 Oldsmobile Cutlass. The grievant had checked the computer printout and determined that the car was not stolen. Nevertheless, he pulled the car over. He asked the driver for his license and insurance, justifying his action on the basis that the man was not wearing a seat belt. The driver was a security guard, with his blue uniform in the back seat and was somewhat irate about being stopped for no reason.

The grievant returned to his car to check on the subject, which took almost thirteen minutes. When the grievant returned to the suspect's car after learning that he was clean, he saw a pistol on the seat next to the driver. He then drew his own gun, a 10 mm semiautomatic Colt Delta Elite, and yelled to the suspect to get out of the car and stay away from the pistol. Then, he pointed his gun at the driver and repeated his instructions. When the driver reached for his gun, the grievant shot him. The grievant said he fired because he was afraid that the driver would shoot him. When the driver jumped head first out of the window on the passenger side, the grievant continued shooting into his buttocks.

There were several witnesses to the shooting. One was a sergeant on the University of Houston Police Force. Also, several university students were at the scene, as were several others. They testified that the grievant fired four or five shots at the suspect. The suspect ran a few steps away from the car, then fell to the ground. A subsequent autopsy showed that the driver was hit eight times, half when seated in the car and half when attempting to run away. The arbitrator's award carefully described the exact angles of each shot to show when it occurred and what the driver was doing at the time to demonstrate conclusively that the grievant was firing at a fleeing suspect who was posing no threat. The applicable rules prohibited police officers from discharging firearms except to protect themselves or another person "from imminent death or seriously injured." This was the policy based on a principle that the Houston chief of police said reflected the importance of human life, that officers could only use deadly force as protectors of life, part of a more defensive approach adopted by the department several years earlier.

The grievant in this case had a bad record, with four prior incidents, two of which involved fatal shootings, each involving a black man. In the latter cases, grand juries refused to prosecute. In fact, a criminologist called as an expert witness by the City testified that these three killings indicated a "propensity to kill people."

The grievant based much of his defense on a theory contained in a text book previously used by the department, *Street Survival*, which instructed police, in cases of physical threat, to keep shooting.

"However, many shots are necessary, you should keep shooting— fast and accurately—until the suspect ceases to be a threat."

But, under Lee Brown, a basic change had occurred in the deadly force policy of the Houston department: there was a greater concern for human life. Now, officers were expected to protect themselves, not to concentrate on shooting the suspect. In this case, the grievant was out of step with the times, as well as being a thoroughly dangerous person.

WHY OFFICERS DON'T REPORT CASES OF EXCESSIVE VIOLENCE

A Fort Worth, Texas officer was disciplined for not reporting an incident in which his partner had stopped the patrol car and had attempted to choke a handcuffed juvenile prisoner in the back seat. The grievant had been involved in a previous incident in which he had slapped one of the occupants in a stolen car, and his fellow officers, who had failed to report the incident, had not been penalized.

The arbitrator, Wallace B. Nelson, pointed out that officers work together and have to depend on each other. That dependence may involve life and death decisions. "Reporting your partner for rules violations does little to improve your relationship." Thus, it is difficult to decide when an infraction should be reported.

In this case, Nelson upheld the five day suspension because he felt that the use of force on a prisoner in handcuffs was so egregious a violation of the rules that it should have been reported. He did offer the further suggestion that the rules needed to be clarified, and he encouraged the police chief to consult with police officers in that connection.

A QUESTION OF PROOF

In a San Antonio, Texas case a police officer was given a fifteen day suspension for kicking a suspect who another officer had arrested and who was lying on the ground on his stomach, with his hands handcuffed behind his back. The grievant was a six year veteran with a clean record.

According to the arbitrator's opinion, the suspect, a mental patient on leave, had been throwing things at vehicles traveling on a highway. When the arresting officer approached him, he came toward him with a board, but when the officer pulled his weapon, the man submitted to being spread-eagled against a barrier, handcuffed, and placed on the ground. While the arresting officer interviewed some complainants, the grievant approached the suspect and kicked him several times in the upper body. There was no evidence that the suspect was resisting or struggling at the time. The arresting officer did not see the incident, but it was reported by another officer on the scene and a civilian who was driving by on the highway. Also, the suspect later complained to the arresting officer that he had been kicked.

The grievant denied having kicked the suspect, but, based on the testimony of the two witnesses, which was corroborated by the suspect, arbitrator William Detwiler concluded that the kicking had taken place, and that it constituted unnecessary physical violence against a prisoner that violated Rule 3.26 of the San Antonio Police Department, which constituted just cause for the discipline.

THE RISK OF MAKING A MISTAKE

Sometimes a police officer may be criticized for failing to take action in circumstances where judgment had to be exercised. Seemingly innocent choices can lead to unexpected outcomes that reflect upon the officer. An example of a situation where a police officer made such a decision in the line of duty is illustrated by a Nevada case. The grievant was a six year veteran of the police department, who had spent over four years driving the paddy wagon in downtown Reno.

At 6:00 PM on October 28, 1987 another officer had been called to a gas station in the downtown area to check on an Indian woman who had gone into the restroom about an hour earlier and had not come out. She had locked the door. The responding officer picked the lock and entered the bathroom. The woman was sitting on the toilet, slumped over, with her pants down, reeking of alcohol. He tried to wake her up, yelling, shaking her, pressing his finger against her collarbone. There was no response. She had passed out, so he called the paddy wagon.

The grievant and his partner arrived soon afterwards. The grievant recognized the woman because he had picked her up over a dozen times before. He knew that she was an alcoholic, and he testified later that he had never seen her sober.

After the grievant's partner put ice down the woman's back, she woke up. Without assistance, she walked out of the bathroom and stepped up into the back of the wagon. The grievant asked her where her boyfriend was. She said that he and several others had returned to the Sparks-Reno Indian Colony, and she asked to be taken there.

The grievant told his radio dispatcher that he was taking the woman to the reservation. There were problems with the reception that evening, and the grievant did not receive a response. Nevertheless, he drove to a place in the reservation where there was a school. At that point, the woman asked to be dropped off. She got out of the wagon, thanked the grievant for the ride, and walked away.

The woman subsequently visited several homes, looking for her friend. She met another man, and, with him, continued to wander around, trying to find something to drink. The man took her behind a building and raped her. The woman later testified that she had finished half a bottle of a port wine earlier in the evening. She did not recall passing out in the bathroom or being transported to the reservation. The gas station attendant said that the woman had not appeared drunk, that he did not notice any slurred speech, balance problems, or other signs of intoxication.

The City admitted that officers were expected to use their judgment in such situations but claimed that the woman's level of alcohol, when tested after the rape, showed that she was too drunk to take care of herself.

The grievant was given a one day suspension for failing to follow departmental policy for handling drunks. People were supposed to be held in civil custody when found in public under the influence of alcohol and unable to care for their own health and safety.

The union argued that the grievant should not have been disciplined, because he could not have anticipated that she would be raped and because he knew that she could function while heavily intoxicated. He took time to talk to her and to observe her condition. He returned the woman to her reservation at her request, so that she could rejoin her friends. His judgment was based on his observation of the woman and his years of experience working the paddy wagon.

Arbitrator Anita Christine Knowlton decided that the City had violated the contract when it suspended the grievant, and she upheld the grievance. In her opinion, the woman was not incapable of caring for herself. She woke up soon after the grievant had arrived on the scene, and when he had talked with her, she had responded to his questions. She had asked to be taken to the reservation. The grievant could not have anticipated that she would be assaulted. He had made a reasonable determination that she was not a candidate for protective custody.

Most police officers make similar decisions on a daily basis. The City's policy would require practically every drunk to be placed in civil custody. The prospect of having such decisions subject to a subsequent disciplinary investigation places great stress on the police officer in the field.

JUDGMENT IN THE USE OF WEAPONS

Cops carry guns, and department rules are intended to insure that these weapons are not abused. For example, police officers in New Jersey are not allowed to fire weapons unless their life is being threatened. In one case, several New Jersey cops shot up a car that had been borrowed by some teenagers. They were disciplined, correctly so.

From time to time, these sorts of incidents are publicized, and the subject of police brutality gains media attention. For example, the heavily publicized Rodney King incident in Los Angeles in 1991 attracted nationwide attention, and, when the police officers were acquitted, set off violent riots there and elsewhere around the country.

An officer who ends up injuring someone by accident may be accused of using excessive force, and a complaint filed by the injured person may result in a disciplinary hearing, and, ultimately, a hearing before an arbitrator.

Cops have to be allowed to protect themselves, and they must be able to control their prisoners, but they should not abuse their authority. Police officers are not above the law.

It can be difficult for a police officer to judge how much force is necessary to make an arrest, and at times, an officer has to subdue a dangerous person. Society expects officers to use appropriate force, but how much force is appropriate?

That question is raised in some of the cases in this chapter. Was the use of force appropriate? Can the department justify the disciplinary action that it took against the officer? These cases involve real-life situations and turn on what a particular arbitrator decides is a reasonable response by the grievant in the particular situation.

Various considerations enter into an arbitrator's thinking. A police officer with long seniority and a clean record is often given the benefit of the doubt. Someone whose record includes earlier incidents of bad behavior will be treated more severely. Every grievant drags his own record of behavior along behind him.

A CASE OF ALLEGED POLICE BRUTALITY

In the small town of Cochella, California, about 120 miles east of Los Angeles, a six year veteran of the police force was working a late shift from 3:00 PM to 11:00 PM. At 9:15 PM, the grievant and his partner, a black officer, responded to a call from the Circle K parking lot where two men were fighting. One man was accusing the other of ramming his parked car and trying to drive away.

The grievant's partner separated the two men. One of the men smelled of alcohol and appeared to be drunk. As he was pulled away, the man called the black officer a "nigger" and threw a punch at the officer, who hit the man with his baton, handcuffed him, and pushed him into the patrol car. The prisoner tried to kick the rear window out of the patrol car. At that point, the grievant called for backup, because a crowd was gathering. Several other patrol units arrived. Hobbles were attached to the prisoner's legs, and he was handcuffed, bending him backward in an awkward position. He was taken to the police station and left on the floor in the squad room. Complaining of a broken jaw and a nose bleed, he began threatening the grievant. The grievant told his partner to write up the charges.

The grievant later said that the prisoner attacked him, so that he had to grab the prisoner around the neck, slap him, and push him back into a chair. A few days later, the grievant's partner claimed that the grievant struck the defenseless prisoner four or five times in the face. His sergeant told him to file an official report, which he did, accusing the grievant of striking the prisoner in the face and head.

The grievant's partner also described two other incidents in which the grievant had used excessive force. In one instance, the grievant had arrested someone for disturbing the peace. The prisoner suffered a broken rib and a punctured lung. In another incident the grievant arrested a juvenile for being drunk, and he took the young man to a back room in the station house and beat him.

A senior officer testified on behalf of the grievant. He said that he had seen the grievant in many situations but had never seen him mishandle a prisoner. He thought that the grievant used an appropriate amount of force in handling prisoners.

The original prisoner also testified. He admitted to having been drunk on the night in question. He could not remember the incident in the parking lot but did remember being taken to the station house. He said that the grievant's partner, the black officer, had done nothing, whereas the grievant, he testified, had given him a beating. When he asked for his handcuffs to be loosened, the grievant slammed him down on his face twice, laughing at him. The grievant kicked him, bruising his legs, and shot mace in his face. This continued, he said, for half an hour.

The City charged the grievant with physically assailing a prisoner without justification, while the prisoner was hobbled, incapacitated, and defenseless, a serious breach of the prisoner's rights.

The City asked the grievant to take a lie detector test, which he did, and it indicated that the grievant was telling the truth when he denied hitting the prisoner.

The grievant testified that it was common practice to bring prisoners back to the station. His only other option would have been to ask his partner to take the prisoner to jail. He did not do this because it would have left him alone. He could have been criticized for either decision, so he waited until the next shift to transport the prisoner.

In his defense, the grievant also pointed out that his partner was a rookie. He may not have known what was going on. The grievant reminded the arbitrators that his partner had not even recalled being called a "nigger."

The arbitrator, Lionel J. Goulet, chaired the panel with two party-appointed arbitrators. Goulet is a lawyer, and he said that the case turned entirely on credibility. He pointed out that the reputation of the department was involved, a matter of legitimate concern because the police must command the respect and the confidence of the public. Nevertheless, the arbitrator ordered the City to reinstate the grievant with back pay, because it had failed to prove that the grievant had attacked the prisoner.

This case, which occurred in a community not far from where Rodney King was beaten to the ground, leaves one with an uncomfortable feeling. Here, even the grievant's partner testified that the grievant had beaten this prisoner and other prisoners, and the prisoner himself gave direct testimony. While it is difficult to appraise the credibility of witnesses without actually seeing them testify, the grievant's own partner testified that the grievant had beaten several prisoners. Could it be that the arbitrator was wrong?

ANOTHER CASE OF ALLEGED VIOLENCE

In another case, a female police officer had been charged with excessive force in a civil lawsuit. The complaint was filed by a woman who claimed that she had been beaten by the grievant while she was her prisoner. The City refused to provide a lawyer to represent the grievant, and the union filed a grievance, claiming that the City was obliged to provide an attorney.

The prisoner had been locked up after a fight but she had tried to escape and resisted being returned to her cell. The grievant had used force to subdue her. The City admitted that the grievant was authorized to use reasonable force to maintain security but charged that the grievant used excessive force, thereby releasing it from any obligation to provide her with legal representation in her defense.

The witnesses introduced by the City indicated that the prisoner had been struck many times. They said, however, that the injuries to the woman might have occurred during the earlier fight, but no such injuries were noted when the prisoner was booked. The City concluded that the injuries were probably caused by the grievant.

Peter R. Meyers is an attorney who has represented management and labor but often serves as an arbitrator. After hearing the evidence, Meyers decided that the grievant had a right to representation by the City. The grievant was acting within the scope of her job, where she was in charge of the lockup area and was authorized to use force when a prisoner tried to escape.

It was for the civil court to determine whether or not she had used excessive force. Because the officer had been sued, she had a right to have her lawyer paid for by the City.

A CITIZEN COMPLAINT FROM A TEXAN DENTIST

This case involved a police officer in San Antonio, Texas who had been dispatched to investigate the damage done to a car resulting from an accident in a parking lot. While he inspected the car, a disagreement arose between the car owners, and one of them, a local dentist, was arrested for disorderly conduct.

San Antonio department regulations say that, "Prisoners shall be protected in their legal rights, given humane treatment, and not subjected to verbal abuse or unnecessary physical violence."

The grievant later testified that when he arrived at the scene, the prisoner was already angry and claimed that his car had been damaged while it was parked in a restaurant lot. He had been arguing with the driver of the other car and her father. When the grievant arrived, the dentist started cursing him. The grievant tried to calm him down, but the man is alleged to have physically attacked him.

When the man resisted arrest, the grievant had to use force. Eventually, the prisoner was on the ground and handcuffed. When the grievant's supervisor arrived on the scene, the prisoner said there had been a "tussle," not that he had been assailed.

Cases involving excessive force often involve conflicting testimony. In this case the City disagreed with much of the grievant's testimony. A photograph of the dentist's blood stained shirt was submitted—the one he was wearing on the night in question. The City also submitted a hospital report, dated February 14, 1988 at 3:50 AM, showing that the prisoner had been treated for bruises and scratches. The City said that it was obvious that the grievant had used excessive force.

The dentist testified that the grievant had been in a bad mood from the outset. After examining the damaged car, the grievant had asked, "Is that all there is?" The dentist had responded that he did not like the officer's attitude and asked for his badge number. That was when they had their physical encounter.

Arbitrator William L. McKee directs the Labor and Industrial Relations Institute at North Texas State University. He pointed out that the case turned on credibility. The grievant and the prisoner told entirely different stories. Although both witnesses seemed honest, based on their "scratchy" personalities, it was not difficult for McKee to see how a fight might have developed.

McKee said that he was unable to determine the truth and reduced the suspension from ten to seven days. It seems difficult to evaluate this award as anything more than a compromise.

CITIZEN COMPLAINTS

These three cases involving alleged police violence illustrate the interplay between citizen complaints and grievance arbitration. Police brutality is an exception. Most police officers show respect for people's rights, do not use unnecessary force, and generate few citizen complaints. Also, it must be said, citizens hesitate to file complaints against police officers. It is difficult to determine how serious police violence is as a community problem because of difficulties in gathering statistics. Much of the material is anecdotal.

It is a fact that police officers have opportunities to use violence. They are armed and trained in the use of force. It would be naive to think that some cops do not take advantage of their position. Fortunately, however, police departments are subject to legal restraints, which includes having to defend an officer's behavior before an impartial arbitrator, and at least some Americans are willing to file charges.

An independent commission that studied police violence in Los Angeles after the beating of Rodney G. King on March 3, 1991, came to the conclusion that police officers in that community often used "excessive force."

In view of the national attention that resulted from the Rodney King videotape and the subsequent acquittal, many American communities are reexamining their procedures as to citizen complaints, looking into the practices of their own police departments, and trying to determine what protections have been installed to protect citizens against police brutality.

CHAPTER 3

The Environment of Enforcement Is Risky

This chapter will describe situations in which officers were injured in the line of duty. Danger is often present in a police officer's daily work, whether the officer is intervening in domestic disputes, engaging in a hazardous car chase, or confronting an armed suspect. When cops are injured, the extent of the department's obligation to provide medical assistance or to continue financial support is likely to be tested. What does the collective bargaining contract require?

Some of the cases described in this chapter indicate that injured police officers are not always adequately protected. A police department should assume responsibility for a police officer injured on-duty. Cops have to take risks, and thousands are injured while trying to apprehend lawbreakers, perhaps even more are injured in mundane domestic confrontations. What is the extent of the obligation of the local government to give such an officer economic security and appropriate medical treatment?

If a police officer is injured as a result of an accident on the job, the department will generally cover the officer's medical bill. Should the department also pay the officer's salary? For how long? What if the accident took place while the officer was off-duty?

Sometimes the extent of an injury is not clear at the time of the incident. What if the full extent is not identified for a year or more? The answer may require an arbitrator to define the medical coverage described in the collective bargaining contract. An arbitrator may need to determine the exact meaning of the contract language.

What about stress related trauma that can't be determined until later? Some cops crack under pressure. If a cop becomes unable to perform, is it the result of an injury or general fatigue? Where does the local government's responsibility end? Do we owe cops life-time security?

WHERE TO DRAW THE LINE

Some cases involve situations where the union is claiming that job stress caused mental or physical illness, such that the officer may seem to be malingering. For example, a police officer in Plymouth, Massachusetts, with almost thirteen years on the force (for the last nine he was a dog handler) experienced chest pains and shortness of breath while riding around in his patrol car. He was taken to a local hospital where he was admitted and remained for forty-eight hours. No cardiac problems were identified. He was absent from work for eight days, and his absences were charged to sick leave, not to an on-duty injury.

The officer's union filed a grievance, claiming on-duty injury pay. When the case came before arbitrator James M. Litton, the grievant's doctor testified that his patient's illness resulted from tension and was probably related to his police work.

The officer claimed that his illness was caused by a dispute he was having with the department. Previously, he had been sent a letter telling him that his extensive use of sick leave was being reviewed, and that he was to submit a doctor's note for every future absence. He had filed a grievance. Then he received another letter, telling him to disregard the previous communication, but warning him that his sick time would be monitored for six months. If there was no improvement, he would be required to submit doctor's notes for any further absences. The Plymouth Police Brotherhood claimed that the chief's letter upset the grievant so much that he experienced chest pains, so that his absence was an on-duty injury.

The contract said that an "employee may be absent from duty without loss of sick leave and without loss of pay . . . when he is absent because of sickness, injury, or disability incurred in the performance of his duty."

The union pointed out that Massachusetts courts "do not require a direct connection between the injury in question and a specific police activity unique to law enforcement as a condition precedent to an award of benefits." The police chief's letters were a "specific occurrence in the line of duty which resulted in the injury."

Arbitrator Litton denied the grievance, concluding that the illness was one that was not caused by an on-duty incident. "There is . . . insufficient evidence . . . to conclude that the sickness, injury and/or disability was incurred in the performance of duty. There is no medical evidence . . . that the officer's chest pains resulted from the stress caused by [the chief's] correspondence with [the officer]."

The Town's doctor may have inadvertently encouraged the union to think that it might win this case. At first, he had indicated that the illness was work related. Later, he changed his opinion, concluding that there was no causality.

What seems odd about this case is that the town neither participated in the hearing or filed a brief, even though it was represented by an attorney. The issue seems significant. If the town had to pay for every illness that occurred while officers were at work, the exposure would seem substantial. Why didn't the town fight harder? In any case, the union lost. The arbitrator concluded that the chest pains that the grievant had suffered were no more than a "coincidence of timing."

HOW TO DEFINE "INJURED"

A police department may argue that stress-related emotional illness is not covered by its medical coverage as the city of Cincinnati did in a case where a police officer was hospitalized in a psychiatric unit, suffering from job-related emotional illness. He was unable to work for several months. The collective bargaining contract said that when a police officer was injured or disabled while in the performance of duty, he is "acting within the scope of employment and should be compensated."

There was conflicting medical testimony. The officer's psychiatrist said that the grievant's condition was "job-related" but did not explain the connection between the condition and the officer's duties, and a police psychologist said that the emotional problems had been present for some time. In his opinion, the recent murder of a fellow police officer might have aggravated the grievant's condition, but the police psychiatrist thought that alcohol and chronic depression also may have contributed to the grievant's condition.

While it appears certain that the grievant's career contributed to his mental illness, there seems to be no question that his condition has been present for some time and does not come under the requirements of the injured with pay benefits.

The union pointed out that the Ohio code made no distinction between physical and emotional disability while the City based its defense on the distinction between sick and injured, claiming that the word "injured" implied only physical injuries, not mental illness.

Arbitrator Joseph Krislov, a professor at the University of Kentucky who had arbitrated labor cases for many years, pointed out that the job injury provision had been adopted in 1970 to accommodate a new city ordinance. Thus, the ordinance provided the key to its meaning. Based on the City's own testimony, he concluded that mental illness was intended to fall within the coverage of the contract provision.

Krislov explained that the ordinary meaning of "injury" extends beyond the merely physical. The City's position, that an officer with a mental condition is ineligible for benefits, was unreasonable. When the City conceded that the grievant's activities as a police officer caused his mental illness, it followed that he should receive the benefit.

Krislov found a causal connection and upheld the grievance. He grounded his decision on five separate points. First, the ordinance adopted by the City said that officers who became disabled in the performance of their duties were entitled to benefits, and the parties intended to incorporate that language in their contract. Second, the City drafted the language. Any ambiguity must be resolved against the drafter. Third, several dictionaries broadly define the term "injured," extending it beyond the mere physical. Fourth, the City's emphasis on sections in the contract dealing with off-duty events was not relevant. And fifth, the grievant's illness resulted, at least in part, because he felt responsible for his friend's death. The grievant had seen his friend die in April, began visiting a psychologist about his sense of guilt in May, entered the hospital in September, and showed suicidal tendencies soon afterward.

HEART ATTACK OR PANIC ATTACK?

Sometimes, rather than mental illness, a police officer will exhibit symptoms that appear to indicate a heart attack but which were finally determined to be caused by stress or panic. Then the issue is whether the anxiety is job related. This disorder mimics cardiac arrest and includes sharp chest pains, dizziness, profuse sweating, and a sense of doom. Panic attacks are an anxiety disorder that is often misdiagnosed by doctors. Many people have such an illness at some point in their lives, and it seems particularly common among police officers, who sometimes encounter severe stress. A common response of people who suffer from panic attacks is to become fixed on the idea that they are suffering heart failure, and they become disabled. For a police officer, this can lead to extensive time away from the job. The question is often whether or not the city should be responsible for such lost time.

A case from Warren, Rhode Island raised that issue. In November 1988, a police officer from that attractive town on Narragansett Bay drove his car to Providence on an errand relating to a cushion and canvas business that he ran on the side. He began to suffer symptoms that he thought might be a heart attack. He entered the Rhode Island Hospital for observation and was released later with a diagnosis of having suffered anxiety attacks. During the following year, he experienced similar symptoms, both on- and off-duty.

In the spring of the following year, he asked the Town to pay him fifty-four days of back pay for the time he had been unable to work because of his illness. He claimed that his condition was caused by "job-related stress." The Town refused to pay, and he filed a grievance. The arbitrator had to decide whether or not the disorder was job-related.

The collective bargaining agreement said that "job-related injuries or job-related absences shall not be deducted from the officer's 'sick leave' allotment," but that the officer must demonstrate a causal connection between the illness and the job duties.

The grievant had worked for the Town of Warren since 1973. Starting as a part-time reserve officer, he became full-time in 1979. He also operated the marine cushion and canvas repair business out of his home.

At the arbitration hearing, the union argued that the grievant had worked under stress. Even his marital and drinking problems were related to job experiences. He drank to suppress his concern about his job, which included life-threatening confrontations which the grievant described. They included a shooting incident where he saw the left side of a woman's face blown away and various other shootings that took place while he was on patrol. He testified that he was repelled by violence, particularly against women and children, and on almost every tour of duty, he said, his job required him to respond to domestic disputes.

The grievant's stress counselor testified that the illness was connected to the officer's job. He warned that all of the symptoms would return if the officer returned to police work. According to him, "the psychological effect related to the onset of panic attacks resulted from a heightened awareness of the grievant's own mortality, coming at a time in his life when he was making a greater commitment to himself and his family." This, the counselor concluded, logically persuaded the grievant that police work was not compatible with his family responsibilities, since police officers are required to "put themselves in potentially life threatening situations every day." He had advised the grievant to look for another line of work.

The Town's medical expert said that, although the grievant may have been dissatisfied with his job, he was not suffering from a stress disorder at the time of his examination. He pointed out that the grievant's job experiences were not unusual and that police officers are expected to cope with such situations.

Arbitrator Katherine B. Overton decided that the grievant's stress disorder was not job-related, as required by the contract. There was no causality between the illness and the police work, and no specific traumatic incident triggered the illness. The grievant's police work may have aggravated his condition, making his occupation inappropriate, but it was not the cause of his illness. She dismissed the grievance.

This arbitration required three separate hearings in February, March, and April of 1990, followed by post-hearing briefs. The Town contested arbitrability initially, arguing that the matter should have been resolved in court because it turned on an interpretation of a state law. Overton's twenty-three page opinion carefully reviewed the evidence and the medical opinions in reaching the determination that the grievant's illness was not job related.

A TRUE HEART ATTACK

In another case, the grievant's chest pains turned out to be a heart attack. The officer was taken to a hospital in an ambulance after complaining that he was not feeling well. He had suffered an inferior myocardial infraction with arteriosclerotic heart disease while on-duty. He was discharged from the hospital seven days later and returned to work during the following month.

The collective bargaining contract said that, "Employees injured during the performance of their duties for the employer and thereby rendered unable to work for the employer, will be paid the difference between the employee's regular pay and workmen's compensation insurance payments."

The officer's union, Law Enforcement Labor Services, alleged that the heart attack was an injury received during the performance of the officer's duties. The stress he encountered on the job was the primary contributing factor to the grievant's condition. On the day of the heart attack, the grievant had engaged in a "heated discussion" with a co-worker.

The City took the position that the grievant was not eligible, pointing out that duty pay has never been paid when a workmen's compensation claim was denied by the insurance company. This was not spelled out in the contract but had been past practice. Officers were only paid when their injury was work related.

Arbitrator John F. Perretti examined the language of the contract as well as the bargaining history. He decided that because of the past practice, he had to deny the grievance.

AN OFF-DUTY INJURY RELATED TO AN EARLIER ON-DUTY INJURY

The earlier cases all related to illnesses or injuries occurring while the police officer was on-duty. Are criteria different when the incident happens while the officer is off-duty? A seemingly trivial case from New Bedford, Massachusetts raised exactly that issue. Could a grievant collect medical expenses for an off-duty injury that aggravated a prior injury that occurred during work?

The grievant was a female patrol officer. In November 1986, while assisting a medic transporting someone suffering from a drug overdose, she injured her right leg. The police department carried her as injured on-duty for six weeks, paying her medical bills even after she resumed her regular police duties.

On August 22, 1987, while off-duty, she twisted her right knee and was unable to walk. She went to the same doctor who treated her original injury, who submitted a $30.49 bill for the examination and medication. The police department refused to pay because the accident happened while she was off-duty.

The contract language was somewhat ambiguous but seemed to be limited to on-duty injuries. The City claimed that the state law gave it discretion whether or not to pay. An employee's only remedy would be to sue the City. The union filed a grievance.

The arbitrator, Alfonso M. D'Apuzzo, dismissed the City's position as "harsh, nonsensical, and absurd," especially since the amount of money was so small. An experienced arbitrator, D'Apuzzo held that "absent clear and unambiguous language, a viable past practice, or an enlightening history of bargaining relating to the subject matter, the arbitrator is constrained to conclude that the parties did not intend such a harsh and unintelligent result." He ordered the City to pay the bill.

Why did a squabble over such a small amount of money require arbitration, with both parties hiring attorneys, participating in hearings, filing briefs, and a ten page arbitration award? Perhaps the parties needed to have the issue resolved so that the City would know whether or not it would have to pay similar medical bills in the future.

AGAIN, THE ISSUE OF CAUSALITY

On May 15, 1987, a Cleveland police officer responded to a domestic violence call. While arresting the suspect, he was struck several times in the head. He felt no need for medical treatment. Several months later, the officer developed severe headaches. In spite of treatment, they only got worse. Eventually, he was hospitalized for neurological disorders and depression. On August 19, 1987, he underwent surgery for the removal of a brain tumor. In January 1988, the grievant returned to light duty for six months. On March 27, 1989, more than a year after the incident, he claimed hazardous duty injury status for all of his time away from work.

The contract required that such a claim be confirmed by both the safety director and the medical director, as well as by the officer's private physician. When the City rejected the claim, the Patrolman's Association filed an arbitration to determine whether or not the claim was covered by the contract. If so, the City would have to pay the grievant's salary, rather than the lesser amount of accumulated sick time.

The City argued that there was no proof that the brain tumor was caused or aggravated by the blows to the grievant's head on May 15, 1987. The City's medical director and a neurologist were of the opinion that the incident had not caused the tumor. The City pointed out that it already had provided sick leave, overtime, furlough, and vacation days, and that this was enough.

The union had tried to convince the City's medical director that the grievant's brain tumor was aggravated by the incident on May 15, 1987. Written reports were submitted from the grievant's doctor at a Cleveland clinic and from another doctor who examined the grievant in connection with a worker's compensation claim. Both doctors had concluded that the injury aggravated a preexisting condition, resulting in continuous and painful headaches. The union pointed out that the medical director had not made a final determination until late in March. The door had been left open for additional medical evidence.

Arbitrator Morlee A. Rothchild, a practicing lawyer, upheld the grievance. She denied the City's claim that the grievance had not been filed on time, because of the City's delay in taking a definitive position. The grievant had been asked to provide additional medical evidence to substantiate his claim for injury pay.

The written reports from the grievant's doctors supported a causal connection between the assault and the officer's brain tumor. Rothchild said that "greater weight should be given to the doctors that actually treated and examined the grievant." Those doctors were more likely to reach an accurate medical assessment of the situation than the employer's doctors, who merely based their opinion on medical reports. When a conflict exists between medical opinions, the medical evidence of the grievant's private doctor should not be ignored unless some contrary evidence is offered to overcome that opinion.

IS HYPERTENSION JOB RELATED?

In a Massachusetts case involving the Town of Hudson, a police officer suffering from hypertension was refused on-duty injury leave even though the department had awarded him such leave several years earlier. In 1985, he had been granted on-duty injury leave for hypertension. Then, in February 1987, he again needed several weeks for treatment of hypertension and high blood pressure. This time, the police department charged his absence to disability leave at a reduced rate. When he complained, the chief explained that a recent court decision now required claimants to show that the hypertension was work related.

The grievant's union, Local 363 of the International Brotherhood of Police Officers, argued that the 1985 incident provided a precedent, since the Town had recognized hypertension as an on-duty injury. A Massachusetts court had recently held that aggravated and repeated injuries previously found compensable under the statute continue to be compensable. The hypertension in 1987 was a repetition of the same illness in 1985. The Brotherhood claimed that job stress caused the hypertension, based on the grievant having bruised his elbow during an arrest, having to work split shifts, and being required to conduct hazardous prisoner checks.

The Town based its refusal on another recent court case that required claimants to prove that their hypertension was job related. In the absence of such proof, the grievant was not entitled to on-duty injury benefits. The Town pointed out that the grievant had been subject to various other sources of stress, for example he had served as president and vice president of the Brotherhood for many years and he also ran a private business. These functions could have been equally stressful.

Arbitrator Mark Santer, a law professor at Northeastern University, decided that under Massachusetts law the grievant was obliged to show a connection between his illness and his duties. He dismissed the grievance, discounting the union's various theories, concluding that checking prisoners was not stressful and pointing out that the grievant had reported for duty on the day following his bruised elbow and that he had been offered the option of daytime shifts.

The union had failed to prove that stress on the job caused the hypertension, and the Town's payment for the prior illness was not relevant because of the intervening Vaughan decision that changed the applicable law. Because of these factors the Town had correctly limited the grievant to disability benefits rather than on-duty injury leave.

JOB-RELATED STRESS

A police sergeant in Middletown, Ohio became unable to work during the early summer of 1989, and the department placed him on sick leave. The officer wanted most of those days converted to injury leave, which paid a higher rate, but this was denied by the injury leave committee. The officer's union filed a grievance claiming that the grievant's absence was due to job-related stress, which was equivalent to an injury in the line of duty. At issue was whether or not job-related stress was covered under the collective bargaining contract.

The union argued that the grievant had "sustained a psychological injury while on the job which caused him to be unable to perform his duties." An extensive psychological report was filed on behalf of the grievant showing incidents of stress, including one where the grievant's wife caught him having sex with a prison matron. The contract did not define injury, so the union relied on Ohio court opinions that recognized emotional distress as an injury. The union claimed that the contract covered emotional distress that was job-related.

The City argued that the contract only covered an officer who was injured in the line of duty, and suffered a single injury occasioned by a specific act or event. The City pointed out that it provided liberal sick leave, which gave adequate protection to officers who became ill. Injury leave should be limited to an on-duty injury that keeps an officer from work.

Arbitrator Frank A. Keenan analyzed the contract, and he noticed that the contract made several references to the "injury" or the "occurrence." He agreed with the City, stating that the officer's illness, at best, was the consequence of the cumulative weight of many occurrences or events, such as strained relationships with co-workers and strained relationships with superiors. On that basis, he denied the grievance. The job-related stress was not an injury covered under the contract, because it was not caused by a single event.

MAY POLICE OFFICERS REFUSE A DANGEROUS ASSIGNMENT?

Police officers are exposed to a wide range of dangers. For example, on October 20, 1987 two Philadelphia deputy sheriffs were told to transport several prisoners from the county prison to court for arraignment. They were told that one of the prisoners had the HIV virus. One of the officers called his supervisor to discuss the situation. Having recently returned to work after a bout with cancer, he was concerned about his safety and that of his family. He was told to transport the other prisoners and return to his office.

When the two officers got back to their office, their supervisor told them that a policy promulgated by Mayor Goode required services to be provided without regard to the fact that a person had AIDS. The officers again expressed their concern about the infected prisoner. They were frightened. The supervisor told them that they should "do what they have to do," but for the record, he was ordering them to transport the prisoner. They refused, and the supervisor directed two other deputies to bring the prisoner to court, which was done without incident.

A few days later, the first two officers were charged with refusing to obey a direct order from their supervisor. After a hearing on October 29, 1987 they were suspended without pay for one day for insubordination.

At a subsequent arbitration hearing before arbitrator Thomas J. Ryan, a 72-year-old former industrial relations manager at Lukens Steel, the Fraternal Order of Police acknowledged that police officers were obliged to obey the orders of their supervisors and that as a general rule, all employees are expected to follow orders.

Normally, the "work now, grieve later" rule demands obedience to orders. No refusal need be tolerated by an employer. However, there is one exception. In *How Arbitration Works* (4th Ed., BNA, pp. 713–716), the Elkouris point out that an employee is not required to comply with an order when the employee reasonably believes that such performance will involve an unnecessary risk of personal injury.

The City argued that the grievants would not have been exposed to any risk in transporting a prisoner with the HIV virus to the courtroom. It was the department's duty to bring the prisoner to trial. The grievants should have done what they were told to do rather than refuse just because they were afraid they might become infected by AIDS.

The arbitrator did not share the City's view of the case. Furthermore, Ryan thought it unlikely that the circumstances of this case would ever be repeated, since by the time of the hearing, the hysteria over AIDS was a thing of the past.

One of the grievants had testified at the hearing that no equipment had been available for handling prisoners with AIDS, such as rubber gloves, masks, or shackles, which he thought were necessary for transporting the prisoner. The arbitrator said that he could appreciate the grievants' concern when placed in historical context. As the City's medical witness explained during his testimony, AIDS hysteria was sweeping the country at the time of the incident and the average person was incapable of sorting out truth from fiction about this still relatively unknown disease. That witness was a board certified internist and a member of the City's AIDS Task Force.

According to the arbitrator, the grievants could not be expected to be informed about AIDS and their job puts them at risk. "The average citizen's contact with an AIDS infected individual is both coincidental and peaceful, whereas the grievants are required to transport a prisoner with AIDS, who could prove to be violent."

In October 1987, when the incident occurred, the department had no program for informing its employees about AIDS. There was an Executive Order, No. 4-86, by Mayor Goode, prohibiting discrimination on the basis of AIDS in providing city services. This was the so-called "policy" that the supervisor had described to the grievants, but there had been no effort by the City to educate employees about AIDS. The Mayor's policy on AIDS had never been explained to the deputies.

Later, an AIDS education program was established, and deputies were given an opportunity to discuss the subject. There have been no subsequent refusals to transport prisoners with AIDS. Officers were furnished with plastic gloves, masks, and shackles.

The arbitrator concluded that the grievants were entitled to think that transporting the HIV prisoner could endanger their health. That belief was induced by the AIDS hysteria that existed at that time. Had the City's subsequent AIDS program existed in October 1987, no deputy would have refused to transport prisoners with AIDS, or at least, there would have been no basis for such a refusal. Under the circumstances, the arbitrator determined that the grievants had a reasonable basis to refuse to carry out the order. Their grievance was upheld, with the suspension to be expunged from the officers' records.

SUMMARY

In this chapter most of the cases have involved disputes about whether or not police departments must continue to pay officers who have been injured or have suffered an illness as a result of their work. Police departments expect their officers to confront danger and to engage in hazardous work but they are not always willing to pay their medical expenses or pay their salaries when they are injured.

These cases, where officers were injured or subjected to stress and then denied full compensation or medical benefits, were submitted to arbitration because the parties interpreted the language of their collective bargaining contracts in different ways. Sometimes they turned on the facts of the case, sometimes on the meanings of particular words or phrases in the contract, or sometimes even on court opinions, but all of these cases illustrate that police officers often encounter danger and occupational stress.

CHAPTER 4

Working with Dangerous Equipment

Police officers spend much of their time in patrol cars, but not every cop is a competent driver. Therefore, accidents do occur. This was the case in Charlovoix County, Michigan where a deputy sheriff, who was an excellent police officer, caused a series of collisions while on patrol. Unfortunately, he had had many accidents, dating back to October 16, 1981, which cost his department a substantial sum of money.

The most recent accident occurred on December 20, 1988 when according to the police report, the officer had been responding to an emergency call. He hit some "black ice" and slid off the road into a snow bank, hitting a utility pole. The damage to the vehicle was $734. The investigating traffic officer did not charge the officer with fault, although it was his ninth accident in seven years.

The department was concerned about how to deal with the officer's chronic problem and asked other departments how they handled similar problems. They said that they sent such officers back to driving school. The department's insurance carrier threatened to cancel the department's coverage unless the officer received similar retraining.

On December 30, the officer was ordered to attend precision driving school for the second time and to submit to a psychological examination to see whether or not any underlying problems were causing his unusual series of accidents. He was also told that he would have to cover the cost

of future accidents. In addition, the department gave him a written reprimand.

In response, the union filed a grievance, pointing out that the accident
was not the officer's fault. Also, the union pointed out that there was no
procedure for giving psychological examinations. The union claimed that
such a test would stigmatize the officer in the eyes of other employees.

Arbitrator Mario Chiesa was asked to decide whether or not the City
had just cause to discipline the grievant. In his award, he noted that there
was no evidence that the grievant was at fault. Chiesa recognized the
department's legitimate concerns about the unfortunate series of accidents,
but, he said, it was interesting that the grievant had never had an off-duty
accident.

The arbitrator upheld the grievance, ordering that the reprimand be
removed from the grievant's file. Since the grievant had already attended
driving school by the time the arbitration hearing was held, that part of the
grievance was moot. For some reason, Chiesa did not resolve the psychological examination issue. Perhaps that had also taken place.

This case was unusual in that the Michigan Law Enforcement Union,
Teamsters Local 214, was represented by an attorney, whereas the
Charlovoix County Board of Commissioners was not. The sheriff himself
represented his department. Employers are represented by lawyers more
often than are police unions. One wonders whether or not the department
expected to lose the case.

ANOTHER CASE OF NEGLIGENT DRIVING

Another driving accident involving a female patrol officer occurred on
the evening of January 27, 1989 in the City of Reynoldsburg, Ohio while
the officer was on-duty. She was suspended for one day without pay. The
question presented to the arbitrator was whether or not giving her a
suspension was fair because it was unclear whether or not she was at fault.

The grievant was driving a police van while on the look-out for a man
who had threatened someone with a gun and she thought that he might be
armed. The grievant knew where the suspect lived because she had been
involved with him once before in connection with a domestic dispute. In
that incident, he had acted violently.

As she approached the suspect's house, she saw him standing in his
driveway with his hands in his pockets. A pickup truck was parked near
the front of his house.

She was driving very slowly, less than fifteen miles per hour when a car
pulled into the street behind her. It flashed its lights and honked, indicating

that the driver wanted to pass. She decided to let the car pass because she did not want it to be caught in a cross-fire. Accordingly, she veered to the right and ran into the parked truck, causing $2,000 worth of damage to her van and $1,000 damage to the other truck. As it turned out, the suspect was not armed.

She admitted at the hearing that her attention was not on her driving, rather it was on the suspect who she thought was carrying a gun. She did not receive a traffic citation, perhaps because it was the policy of the police department not to ticket officers for such offenses.

The City investigated the incident. The accident was reported in the press and cost the City its $500 deductible. The grievant's union, the Fraternal Order of Police, argued that she should not have been suspended even for a day because she was facing a hazardous situation that involved people in the neighborhood as well as herself. Gunfire might have been anticipated.

Arbitrator Donald B. Leach had to decide whether or not her suspension was appropriate. In examining the contract, he noted that it required progressive discipline, including a warning, a written reprimand, and suspension before an officer could be subject to demotion or termination. Leach pointed out that the grievant had not been reckless. At most, she had been negligent. He concluded that the penalty was too harsh. He modified the suspension to a written reprimand and ordered the City to pay the grievant for the day she had not been allowed to work. By the date of the hearing, this grievant had already participated in a defensive driving course.

This is another case which involved a minor dereliction and a minor penalty. Again the union was represented by a lawyer while the chief of police represented the department. This case illustrates the day-to-day pressure on police officers, responding to a complaint involving a dangerous individual who may be armed. Is it any wonder that the grievant in this case was keeping her eyes on the suspect and collided with a parked vehicle as a result?

BARRICADING AN ESCAPE ROUTE

Anyone who watches television is familiar with police officers who use their patrol cars to close off streets to stop criminals so that they can be apprehended. In the city of Fort Worth, Texas, as in other places, this procedure violates the code of conduct for police officers, which prohibits using a police vehicle to barricade a street.

On Wednesday, August 31, 1988 an officer responded to a robbery call. After obtaining a description of the suspect, he began searching nearby apartment buildings. At about the same time, other officers began to pursue a motorcycle. As the motorcycle traveled west on Ephriham Avenue, the grievant entered the intersection with his patrol car. The motorcycle collided with his patrol car, causing damage to both vehicles and critically injuring the driver of the motorcycle. The City later claimed that the officer positioned his car to barricade the street to stop the motorcycle. If the officer had placed his police vehicle in the path of the motorcycle, he would have violated the rule against using a police vehicle as a barricade. The officer was suspended for five working days.

His union filed a grievance, claiming that the City had failed to prove that the grievant intended to use his car as a barricade and that he was only crossing the intersection to search the apartment complex on the other side. It was relevant, the union pointed out, that his overhead lights were not turned on, because he would have turned on his overhead lights if he were attempting to barricade the road. The grievant did not know about the pursuit. He testified that he had not heard any radio calls about the chase, nor was there a record of his calling the dispatcher or offering his assistance.

The officer said that he first saw the motorcycle just before the impact and that he never did see the police chase vehicle. When he saw the motorcycle, he slammed on his brakes in an effort to avoid an accident rather than speed across the intersection.

Arbitrator Elvis C. Stephens had to decide whether or not the officer intended to barricade the road. Intent was required for there to be a violation of the code. Stephens concluded that the evidence did not show that the grievant intentionally barricaded the intersection to stop the motorcycle. The light was poor; the motorcycle was traveling at about 80 miles per hour. He decided that the suspension should be revoked.

RESPONSIBILITY FOR COMMUNICATIONS EQUIPMENT

Police departments are understandably concerned about damage to their patrol cars, and there is other expensive equipment being used in law enforcement, particularly since communications and computerized information systems have come into vogue. Police officers are responsible for their valuable equipment, and when it is stolen, the police department may decide to discipline the officer.

For example, in the town of Warrensville Heights, Ohio on January 9, 1989 a police officer reported to work for the late night shift. The temperature was about 20°F. He could not get into his patrol car from the driver's side because the lock was frozen, but he was able to enter from the passenger side. The officer was equipped with a radar unit, a camera, and a shotgun. He placed the radar unit on the floor, in front of the passenger seat. After driving around on patrol, he was dispatched to the scene of a disturbance. Other police cars had already arrived. He got out of his car, locking the door on the driver's side with the inside lock over the arm rest. After leaving the car, he participated in handling the situation. After the incident was over, the officer responded to another call. At around 12:30 AM, he noticed that his radar unit was missing.

The radar unit was never found, and the equipment cost $500 to replace. The detectives who investigated the theft found no evidence of forced entry and never apprehended the thief. They concluded that the loss was due to the officer's carelessness. The officer was suspended for one day and required to reimburse the City. The Police Benevolent Association filed a grievance.

Arbitrator Marvin J. Feldman had to decide if there was just cause to discipline the officer or to charge him for the City's loss. Feldman determined that there was no standard operating procedure for checking door locks. Even though the department required officers to "be careful in the use of all city property," Feldman decided that it was unfair to expect an officer on an emergency call to double check door locks before leaving a cruiser. He also discovered that these patrol cars had a chronic problem with frozen locks.

It seemed reasonable to Feldman that this grievant should be more concerned with public safety and about his fellow officers than he was about the radar set left in the cruiser. Since there was evidence that the locks were frozen, the City should accept liability. The arbitrator upheld the grievance.

ACCIDENTAL DISCHARGE OF AN AUTOMATIC WEAPON

Another common mishap in police work is the accidental discharge of firearms. Should the responsible officer be disciplined? How serious is such an infraction?

A case involving the discharge of a weapon occurred in Chicago on May 1990, when a patrol officer noticed two women and a man arguing. He got out of his car to persuade them to stop fighting among themselves and to move them along. When they resisted, the officer decided to arrest the man. One of the women attacked the officer, who then attempted to handcuff her. This prompted the other woman to punch the officer in the face. In the scuffle, the officer's second weapon, a semiautomatic 45 caliber handgun, was pulled from its holster. A shot went off in the air.

The officer had been carrying that gun for almost twelve years. He was aware that semiautomatic handguns were supposed to be carried with the chamber empty and with the hammer all the way down. It was a violation of departmental rules to carry such a gun with a round in the chamber.

The Internal Affairs Division recommended that the officer be reprimanded. This recommendation was shown to the officer when he signed a waiver for a complaint review panel. He knew that the department was not bound by such recommendations but that it usually followed them. When he subsequently learned that the superintendent had increased his penalty to a one day suspension, he asked his union to file a grievance. If he had known what penalty was about to happen, he said that he would not have signed the waiver.

Arbitrator George T. Roumell, Jr. had to decide if the City acted properly when it suspended the grievant. The union admitted that firing a weapon by accident was not insignificant. This was what the superintendent was trying to avoid by enforcing the empty chamber rule. Roumell denied the grievance, and the one day suspension was confirmed.

FIRING INTO THE FLOOR OF THE POLICE STATION

Another case involved an accidental firing of a gun on June 26, 1989 that took place in Redwood City, California, where a police officer, after coming on duty, went to the dressing room to change into his uniform. He took his service revolver out of its holster to make sure it was functioning properly. He emptied the ammunition out of the cylinder, and examined the rounds. He started to reload the weapon, then decided to dry-fire the weapon to make sure it was working properly. He again emptied that cylinder and pointed the muzzle at the floor. He dry-fired once, then fired a live round from his .357 magnum into the floor, breaking one of the tiles. There were other officers in the locker room, but no one was injured. He did get their attention.

The City decided that a one day suspension was appropriate because this was viewed as a serious, and potentially dangerous, act of gross negligence on his part.

The officer's union complained that the punishment was too severe and that his action was merely negligent. The City had no rule that specifically covered the situation where a weapon was fired by accident. The union argued that there was no basis for discipline and that a suspension was too harsh. The grievant offered to make restitution for the tile. The union also suggested that he might benefit from more training in handling his service weapon.

Arbitrator William E. Riker pointed out that the officer's employment record was unblemished. It was clear that while the discharge of the weapon was an accident, the incident was too serious to be treated lightly. "While the incident was unintentional there is no way that '—oops, I didn't know the gun was loaded' can be excused.

"Law enforcement officers place themselves in harm's way every day they put on the blue uniform. Unlike most of the citizenry they serve, they must be ever vigilant and conscious in the handling of firearms, for their weapon is a tool of the profession. Unlike other professions with their own particular tools of the trade, in law enforcement the misuse or careless handling of a police officer's weapon can have dire consequences."

Riker felt that the suspension was reasonable and hoped that the suspension would have some impact and would be retained in the grievant's memory during his future career. The one day suspension was sustained.

SUMMARY

Serving as a police officer involves driving in patrol cars carrying weapons and other activities fraught with danger. Such activities increase the stress on police officers, who never know when they may be involved in a car chase, a serious accident, or an exchange of gunfire. The cases in this chapter show how easy it is to make mistakes and how quickly police departments blame the officer. Being responsible for expensive equipment and carrying dangerous weapons increases the pressure on the individual officer.

In the cases involving the discharge of handguns, the shots went off by accident. That is not always the case. On July 17, 1991 a police officer carried his revolver into Baltimore police headquarters to discuss an accusation that he had abused a ten-year-old girl. He shot and wounded a major and a lieutenant and killed himself. His superiors were taken to the hospital in critical condition. He had been on the force for over twenty years. Police officers carry lethal weapons, and they are accustomed to making use of them. When they are placed under stress, the results can be dangerous to both themselves and others.

CHAPTER 5

Sex and Race Discrimination

Historically, police departments have been predominantly male. Women are a relatively new ingredient in the police environment. Previously, women worked as dispatchers and office workers, but now they have taken to the streets, so to speak, because Department attitudes toward women are changing. It was normal practice for two men to operate as partners in patrol cars, however with women on the force, a man and a woman are likely to share a car. Why not?

The law requires that men and women be treated with equality. Does that mean, however, that assignments should be entirely sex-blind? Do prisoners have a right to be searched by someone of their own sex? Are the constitutional rights of a woman violated when she is subjected to a strip search by a male cop? Or vice versa? Must all relationships between the police and the public be sex-blind? These kinds of factual situations are sometimes raised in arbitration.

As the police become more ethnically mixed, black and white cops are working side by side—something almost unheard of at mid-century. Public service employment has become integrated, and police departments that are not alert to this change and observant of the obligations of the civil rights laws are sued for discrimination. Today almost every collective bargaining contract contains an antidiscrimination provision.

Disputes involving sexual and racial issues continue to surface, however, because actual equality is not achieved with the stroke of a pen, but requires a sustained effort to change deeply ingrained cultural attitudes and operating policies. The cases in this chapter discuss sexual and racial discrimination. The policy in favor of legal equality, expressed in anti-discrimination laws and in departmental policies, is trying to create equality in a police environment that is still marked with discrimination.

The aspirations of civil rights legislation collides with the reality of prejudice. The cop, in such a situation, is again caught in the middle: having to pretend that sex and race have no relevance and that people are neither black nor brown nor white. All of this adds another level of complexity to an already difficult job.

SEX DISCRIMINATION ON THE JOB

Sex harassment sometimes occurs in a police department, as in other jobs. Men impose themselves upon women. Some women complain while others do not. Some men are disciplined while others are excused. Factors that make the situation unique in the police department is that most participants are armed, may have to rely on each other in tense situations, and are engaged in difficult work.

For example, a man and a woman who are required to spend long hours together in a patrol car, day after day, develop an intimacy that can magnify any latent tendency to engage in coercion or sexual harassment. Such a relationship can easily deteriorate into one where charges are made that the male officer has violated the law. A police department, however, that refuses to assign female officers to duty in rotation may be charged with violating its affirmative action obligations.

Such a case arose in Rhode Island. A female deputy marshall became eligible for a coveted overtime opportunity on a Sunday. The work involved transporting male prisoners and required them to be searched. The seniority bidding policy of the department, which had been in effect for many years, had been adjusted so that one male would always be on the team. The shift was offered to one female in the normal way, but the next female applicant, the next officer in the normal order of seniority, would be passed over in favor of a man. The department had a policy of not allowing two women to work together on such an assignment because of the need to search male prisoners. Only two marshalls worked on Sunday, picking up prisoners from various police stations and transporting them to an adult correctional institution in Cranston.

As it turned out, the woman who had been awarded the assignment was, on the following day, offered an even more coveted overtime job in a hospital, so that the grievant had been offered the Sunday detail, but by then, she had made other commitments.

On her behalf, her union filed a grievance. The union said that the adjusted policy constituted illegal sex discrimination and violated the collective bargaining agreement and Rhode Island law. The department said that the policy was reasonable because of the right of male prisoners to be searched only by males.

Past practice was not in dispute. For many years, the service had followed a rigid seniority policy as to Sunday work assignments, and the work was offered to each employee in turn, according to seniority, until all of the assignments were filled.

On January 5, 1989 when a second female officer would have been awarded the transport assignment based on seniority, she was passed over. This was done deliberately, after the duty lieutenant discussed the problem with the marshall. Women were relatively new to the service, having been brought into the deputy position for the first time in 1984.

At the arbitration hearing, the department argued that it was essential to have at least one man on the job. When prisoners are strip searched, they must be searched "to the groin or vaginal area every time," according to the marshall's testimony. Men should be doing the searching on the male prisoners, he said, because the search includes pat downs of a prisoner's whole body, including private areas. Women prisoners were sometimes transported, but, according to the marshall, they were never subjected to a strip search, at least not by his men.

Joan G. Dolan is an active arbitrator in New England. She was asked to decide whether or not the department had violated the seniority provisions in the contract by refusing the grievant an opportunity to work the Sunday transport assignment on January 5, 1989.

She pointed out that the department's own manual required officers to search prisoners for weapons before transporting them. Female deputies were to be used when female prisoners were being transported, whenever available. She noted that the grievant was a well-trained, highly competent officer, and that, as the union had pointed out, police officers constantly searched prisoners on the street without regard to sex.

The arbitrator said that it was clear, beyond any shadow of doubt, that the overtime provisions of the contract were violated. The contract requires overtime to be offered as "equally as possible," and the longstanding practice of offering overtime according to seniority defines the meaning of that term. The department did not present persuasive evidence demonstrating any business necessity for bypassing the grievant. The arbitrator ordered the department to pay the grievant the overtime she otherwise would have earned.

In a final comment, Dolan had this to say: "As so often happens in arbitration, I suspect there are more facts related to this matter than I heard, but the ones I did hear and have outlined seem to indicate an approach in which the situation at issue here is an insurmountable barrier for the women marshalls and no problem for the men. On this record, it is completely unclear to me why that is so. If two women cannot work Sunday detail because of the possibility of strip searching prisoners of the opposite sex, how can two men?"

As this case illustrates, concepts of sexual equality are washing away ingrained cultural values that made it possible to discriminate against women. Few legal barriers remain, particularly in the area of public service. People of both sexes are having to adjust their thinking, because the law requires them to subtract gender from their perception of the working world.

SEX HARASSMENT IN THE STATION HOUSE

With women becoming more frequent in police departments there are new opportunities for unwelcome sexual advances, and consequently there are more complaints from female officers. For example, a female officer on the Corpus Christi, Texas police force complained that a senior officer had hugged and attempted to kiss her. The incident occurred in the hallway of the station house on January 13, 1988. The male officer denied touching the woman on that day. He denied *ever* touching her, except that on one occasion when he "socially hugged" the complainant around the shoulders. There were numerous witnesses present at the time.

The department's investigator ordered the officer to submit a statement. He did not immediately comply, claiming that he was entitled to consult his lawyer. The City called this insubordination. The officer was suspended for ten days, five for sexual harassment and five for insubordination.

Arbitrator Richard F. Dole, Jr., a Professor of Law at Bates College of Law at the University of Houston, teaches labor law and collective bargaining. He decided that the grievant did have a right to consult his lawyer, and he reduced the sex harassment suspension to a warning letter, pointing out that the grievant was a senior officer with an outstanding record.

Dole pointed out that, "Sexual harassment includes unwanted physical contact with a fellow employee of the opposite sex that is not required by official duties. The presence of other people does not preclude sexual harassment. By increasing the visibility of unwanted physical contact and the embarrassment of a victim, the presence of other people can aggravate the offense."

Dole noted that the grievant's embrace was unsolicited, highly visible, and public. Nevertheless, he did not think that publicly hugging a woman without her consent on one occasion should merit anything more than a warning letter, and he so decided.

Similar cases have arisen in other employment contexts, where male executives embrace female employees, thinking that they will be well received. In most cases, the woman does not complain, accepting it as a friendly gesture or not wishing to make an issue of such a relatively trivial matter. Sometimes, a woman may encourage such advances or even initiate them. But, with increased sensitivity to possible sex harassment charges, males are reluctant to engage in behavior that might be misunderstood, particularly in situations where the male is in a position of authority over the female. Presumably, sex harassment will be encountered less frequently as people become more familiar with the new rules of the game.

RACE DISCRIMINATION ISSUES ARE ALSO ARBITRATED

Sex discrimination issues have become more common in police departments as women officers are increasingly employed, but racial disputes have also increased. Police departments are under pressure to hire more minority officers to reflect community ratios. This has augmented the complement of black and Hispanic officers. Job assignments and promotions must accommodate the requirements of Title VII.

After having served for fourteen years on the Philadelphia force, a black detective with an excellent record was transferred to patrol duty. For six years, he had worked with the burglary squad in plainclothes on a fixed work week, a preferred assignment. The officer felt that he had been demoted because of his race.

After learning of the transfer, he returned to the squad room, where he saw a sign saying that officers were needed on patrol. He wrote on the sign: "3 NIGGERS NOW GONE, YOU NEXT." For doing so, he was laid off for twenty days without pay because the City said that the grievant's act constituted conduct unbecoming an officer and that he should be punished. The union filed a grievance, arguing that the punishment was excessive.

A few days after the incident, the black police officers' organization, the Guardians Civil League, had featured it at a press conference. As a result, the incident received media attention. The grievant was not involved in that aspect of the situation except, in a discussion with the head of the Guardians, he neglected to tell him that he wrote the words, leaving the impression that they were written by a white officer.

The department had promised the grievant that if he did not go to the media with his story, he would receive leniency. The City claimed that it did show leniency by not firing the officer. "Humbug," said the union, instead of receiving a slap on the wrist, he was castrated.

Arbitrator Kinnard Lang concluded that the word "nigger" had not been intended as a racial slur but as a protest. He pointed out that the word, like others, derives its potency from its context. Depending on the situation, "nigger" can attract attention or it can encourage bonding. It was a bad choice of words, Lang said, reflecting poor judgment, because it makes some people uncomfortable, regardless of their race.

Arbitrator Lang reduced the twenty day suspension to five days, considering his own view of the incident and the grievant's excellent fourteen year record.

RACIAL SLURS DURING A STRUGGLE

In Fort Worth, Texas a police officer was given a five day suspension for using the word "nigger" while arresting a suspect. The officer had an excellent record and had just survived a particularly dangerous experience.

On July 7, 1990 he and his partner saw a large crowd gathered in a parking lot of the North Fort Worth Bank. They drove into the lot and parked, then both got out and walked toward the crowd. Someone told them that a car had run over several people and was trying to escape. The grievant ran towards the vehicle, a 79 Chevrolet Caprice, as his partner returned to their cruiser. The Chevy stopped outside the lot. The driver, holding a tire iron, and the passenger, a 17-year-old black male, got out of the car. As the grievant approached, the passenger yelled, "Let's get out of here," and both began to get back into the car. The grievant arrived in time, grabbed the passenger by the shirt, and yelled "Police. Don't move," but the man broke loose, got in the car, and closed the door.

The car drove away, with the grievant hanging onto the open window. The passenger told the driver to "scrape the cop off the car." The grievant's partner by now was following the car with his two sirens and emergency light turned on. He noticed that the car was swerving in an attempt to dislodge the grievant.

The passenger in the car was trying to pry the grievant's hands from the door, but the grievant hooked his foot inside the window and managed to draw his revolver. The passenger grabbed it in an attempt to take it from him, but then he changed his mind and told the driver to stop. The officers finally got control of the situation, with the grievant pulling the passenger through the window, with both their hands on the gun, while his partner placed the driver on the ground in handcuffs. In order to get the passenger to release his hold on the gun, both officers had to force him to let go. Finally, the grievant's partner was also able to handcuff the passenger. During this transaction, the grievant referred to the passenger as a "nigger."

The two suspects were charged with aggravated assault on a police officer. During the confrontation, the grievant had cut his arm and jammed his finger.

Ten days later, the passenger and his mother came to the station house to file a complaint that he had been the victim of excessive force and racial slurs. He charged that the grievant had hit him, threw him to the ground, and kicked him, as well as calling him "names as in nigger this and nigger that." The grievant denied hitting, kicking, or handcuffing the passenger, and his partner confirmed his statement. The grievant did not deny that he might have used a racial slur during the confrontation, and his partner confirmed that he had used the word "nigger" during the struggle for the gun.

A review board concluded that the grievant had used a racial slur, and recommended an oral reprimand, but the chief of police decided that a five day suspension was appropriate based on section 703(f) of the Fort Worth police code of conduct that prohibits the use of "words ... which are derogatory ... in nature ... because of their race, color," etc.

The grievant defended his conduct on the grounds that the notice of suspension did not accurately describe the incident, but his body mike was transmitting during the final moments of the chase, and he was recorded as follows:

- On the ground, on the ground, blow your brains out, on the ground.
- God damn nigger.
- Get out of the god damned car, you fucking nigger.

The grievant admitted that it was his voice on the tape.

The chief of police had testified that "nothing that happens in the police department has a more damaging and severe impact on the department than the use of a racial slur in dealing with the public."

On his part, the grievant told the arbitrator that he never would have appealed, if the chief had shown any appreciation for his heroism in connection with the incident. According to him, the fact that he had almost gotten killed seemed to have been obscured by his use of a racial slur.

Arbitrator Norman Bennett denied the appeal on the basis that the grievant had violated a specific rule and that the punishment was reasonable.

A DEPARTMENTAL WITCH HUNT

Police departments do not take these matters lightly. On January 12, 1988 there was a rumor circulating around the Tracy City Police Department that two employees had copulated on the premises; an investigation disclosed later that the rumor was false. The department, however, decided to find out who had initiated and spread the rumor. After a series of interviews, three employees were accused of engaging in gossip and were suspended. Their union, Local 439 of the Teamsters, filed a grievance on their behalf.

Arbitrator Alan R. Rothstein was asked to decide whether or not the employees had been fairly disciplined. He took his assignment seriously, pointing out that such a rumor could be destructive to the persons accused. The department's intense concern did not surprise him.

After hearing testimony, Rothstein concluded that the City had failed to demonstrate that the grievants were the source of the rumor or that any of them had a malicious intent toward the subjects of the rumor. Many people had participated in spreading or discussing the rumor. The grievants did not seem to have participated more than any of the others.

Rothstein went on to criticize the department, explaining that there are better ways to respond to rumors, particularly in a working environment. For example, management could have done more to counteract the rumors, the employees who were initially interviewed could have been told to keep quiet, or attempts to inhibit the circulation of the rumor could have been made. According to Rothstein, punishing someone who spreads a rumor is often counterproductive. In this case, he decided that the employees had been improperly suspended because the department was unable to demonstrate their culpability. They were returned to work with back pay.

SUMMARY

Issues of sex and race discrimination will continue to receive the attention of labor arbitrators. As to women, the pressure and occasional danger that police officers must face and the intimate relationship that builds up between people who are working together will continue to produce situations where female officers will feel exploited or will not be treated with full equality.

Race, too, will continue to generate conflict situations, as departments attempt to integrate larger numbers of minorities into their ranks. So long as race is a factor in the communities that police officers serve, it will produce situations in which race is perceived as the motivation for discriminating actions.

CHAPTER 6

Drugs and Drinking

Some police officers abuse alcohol and drugs, as do many other workers. Some of this activity takes place on the job, but more often, it occurs in private. When this kind of abuse comes to the attention of the police department, the officer may be disciplined or terminated.

To an arbitrator, the morality of an employee's life-style is not relevant. The question is whether or not the activity affects the grievant's duties as an employee. The special role that the police play in the community creates a unique sensitivity to public criticism and imposes a higher standard on police officers. It is difficult to separate an officer's private life from his or her responsibility to serve as a role model, and arbitrators are sometimes obliged to draw that line.

The cases in this chapter involve alcohol and drug abuse. Sometimes, such abuse may be a crime, as when an officer is driving under the influence. In other situations, off-duty misbehavior may violate a departmental rule or may prejudice the department's reputation in the community.

ON-DUTY USE OF MARIJUANA

Marijuana has become the recreational drug of choice for many young Americans. A marijuana case involving a police officer was heard by Linda

Klein, the daughter of arbitrator Peter DiLeone. She has been hearing cases in the Cleveland area since 1981.

On April 16, 1988 a police officer in Middletown, Ohio went to his assigned patrol car shortly before 11:00 PM. The car had last been driven by the grievant, who had worked from 7:00 AM to 3:00 PM and the car had remained in the police parking lot during the following shift.

When the officer turned on the heater, he smelled marijuana, and he reported this to his supervisor. They searched the car but found no marijuana. They discussed the situation with the chief of police, who recalled that during the previous summer another officer's wife had said that the grievant was a marijuana user. Also, the chief recalled that the grievant's productivity had been low according to departmental statistics. Also, the grievant had a high rate of sick leave.

On the basis of that inconclusive evidence, the chief decided that the grievant might be using marijuana. He ordered him to take a drug test. The grievant responded he would not do so without consulting his attorney and his union. Later, he refused to submit to the test. He was suspended for thirty days and told he must submit to random drug tests in the future, "with or without suspicion." He filed a grievance.

Arbitrator Klein had to decide whether or not the chief had reasonable grounds to order a drug test. She was dubious. The odor of marijuana may have created an initial suspicion, but there was inadequate proof. The City could not rely on a rumor generated by another officer's wife nine months earlier, especially because other charges made by that woman turned out to be unfounded. The grievant's record of arrests and tickets had been low, but he was no worse than some other officers.

The arbitrator decided that the City did not have reasonable grounds to order a drug test because its evidence was insufficient. She ordered the suspension to be rescinded and removed from the grievant's record. The City was told to pay him for whatever loss he incurred while suspended.

AN UNEXPECTED RESULT

When departments think that officers are using drugs, they may require urine tests, but those tests are not always reliable. A case from Corpus Christi, Texas, provides an example.

The grievant had served for over twenty years with the police department. His performance had been above average with no challenges about his honesty, integrity, or devotion to duty. On August 22, 1989 the grievant and other officers assigned to narcotics were told to submit urine specimens for drug testing. During the evening before the test, the grievant had taken five milligrams of valium in order to sleep. As he subsequently explained, he had injured his knee in an on-duty motorcycle accident and had a supply of valium that he had acquired when his brother-in-law died several years earlier.

The drug test on the grievant came back positive. On November 22, 1989 he was fired for violating regulations against drug use.The use of valium without a doctor's prescription was illegal but seldom enforced. The City thought it had a good case. Its "zero tolerance" policy was well established. Possession and use of a controlled substance without a prescription issued to the person taking the controlled substance was a violation of departmental rules.

Arbitrator Henry L. Sisk had to determine whether or not the drug violation justified a termination. He decided that the penalty was too harsh. Even though police are held to a higher standard of conduct than other employees, the use of valium should not be treated the same as drugs such as cocaine or marijuana, which are illegal in Corpus Christi. Valium is legal but controlled. The arbitrator decided that a thirty day suspension would be appropriate and ordered the City to pay the grievant for the days he was suspended in excess of thirty days.

In substance abuse cases, the arbitrator's attitude toward the particular drug may influence the decision. Some arbitrators use alcohol, some use marijuana, and some use a variety of prescription drugs. How they regard these various substances is likely to determine how they decide the grievances that are brought to their attention. These attitudes may depend on the age, cultural background, or personality of the particular arbitrator, as well as on the language of the contract, the departmental regulations, and the applicable provisions of the local law.

One further consideration that is applicable in drug cases is that some strict substance abuse criminal laws are seldom enforced. In this case, the arbitrator was influenced by that factor.

THE USE OF MARIJUANA

Another case from Corpus Christi, Texas illustrates how seriously some police departments regard the use of marijuana, and how harshly they punish its use by police officers.

The grievant was a Mexican-American with ten years of service. When transferred to the narcotics division, he was obliged to submit to a drug test. Concerned that the test might reveal his use of marijuana, he decided to confess to a supervisor. He told him that several months earlier, he had gone to Nuevo Laredo, Mexico on a holiday and that after a few drinks at a local bar, he went to a parking lot with some men he met there, some gringos. They sat in a car and passed around a marijuana joint. He told the supervisor that he had taken one drag when it came around to him. The supervisor reported the story to the chief of police.

When the grievant was subsequently tested, three times in all, all three tests were positive, showing major traces of marijuana in the grievant's urine. He was terminated.

The grievant appealed the termination, claiming that the tests were not accurate and that termination was too harsh a penalty.

The City challenged the grievant's story that he only smoked marijuana during a trip to Mexico. If he meant that he had not violated the law because he smoked in a foreign country, his theory was invalid. As a police officer, he should not use marijuana at any time. The high level of the drug THC found in the grievant's urine showed that the grievant's account of having taken one drag of marijuana three months before was patently false.

The union argued that the grievant should not have been terminated because that was unfair. Other employees had not been fired for abusing alcohol. The grievant should be given a second chance and allowed to rehabilitate himself, particularly in view of his seniority.

The arbitrator, Elvis C. Stephens, a professor at the College of Business at North Texas State University, decided that the grievant had been terminated for just cause, and he denied the grievance. When the grievant admitted using marijuana, his supervisor properly informed the department. The three drug tests showed extensive use, indicating that the grievant had violated the police department's rules against the use of drugs. The arbitrator explained that under the collective bargaining contract, he was not authorized to substitute a lesser penalty. The penalty was harsh but not arbitrary or capricious under the circumstances.

Many employers, including police departments, treat the abuse of marijuana more seriously than alcohol abuse. This may reflect cultural attitudes. Marijuana possession and its use is a crime in some communities, whereas the use of alcohol has become largely decriminalized. Marijuana is also considered a "threshold" drug by many people, leading to the use of other criminal substances. This sometimes justifies a less lenient policy toward marijuana.

Often the only way to prove such use is to require urine tests, and then the validity of the test must be demonstrated. Arbitrators have developed generally accepted criteria as to how such tests are to be carried out, relating to the security and the testing of urine samples. Arbitrators usually require that the urine sample be taken in a controlled, supervised environment, that transmission to the laboratory be secure, and that any chemical tests conform to established procedures. If a union believes that the employer has failed to meet those criteria, it can provide its own drug test, based on another sample of the grievant's urine.

DRUG TESTS ARE NOT ALWAYS RELIABLE

Some cases turn on a comparison between drug tests. For example, in Broward County, Florida a female detention sergeant was charged with the use of marijuana, as well as associating with a convicted felon and conduct unbecoming an officer. According to the contract, any one of these violations could have provided just cause for her discharge.

The felon had acted as the informer in the case. After living in the sergeant's home for several months, he claimed that they had smoked marijuana together. By admitting this, he placed himself at risk of prosecution, which the department considered as some indication that he was telling the truth. Based on his statement and on the fact that the grievant had failed a drug test, she was terminated. She filed a grievance.

Both the preliminary test and the follow-up conformity test showed that her urine contained about five times more than the minimum allowable for the preliminary test, and twenty-five times more for the follow-up test. Both tests were administered by the Met-Path laboratory.

The grievant denied using marijuana, challenging Met-Path's ability to properly analyze and test her urine. On the advice of her doctor, she had submitted another urine sample to Smith, Kline laboratories within twenty-four hours. That lab performed a preliminary test that was negative for marijuana.

Arbitrator Marshall J. Seidman, a graduate of Harvard Law School and an experienced arbitrator, had to decide which of the tests to accept. He decided to discount the results of the grievant's test and to rely entirely on Met-Path, pointing out that the Smith, Kline test was not performed in accordance with normal procedures. The grievant had not provided a secure sample. Indeed, the circumstances surrounding the test were suspicious. No nurse was present when the grievant gave her first sample, and there was hot and cold running water in the bathroom, and nothing prevented it from being mixed with the grievant's urine.

To the contrary, Met-Path followed strict procedures, resulting in more reliable results. The water in the toilet was colored, so that it could not be mixed with urine, and there was no running water in the bathroom. A nurse watched the grievant produce her urine sample. Nor was the grievant allowed to drink water just before giving the sample, which might have thrown off the test.

Arbitrator Seidman dismissed the grievance, concluding that the grievant had used marijuana, which, according to the contract, was just cause for her termination.

A MITIGATED CASE OF COCAINE USE

Police departments tend to treat the use of cocaine with even more severity than marijuana. For example, in Lawrence, Massachusetts a police officer was fired after admitting to having used cocaine on two occasions. He claimed mitigating factors, asserting that he should not have been terminated, and his union filed for arbitration.

As a police officer, his record had been outstanding, and he had received several commendations. At the arbitration hearing, his captain testified in his favor. He had never been disciplined before his discharge.

The City learned of the grievant's cocaine use as a result of an investigation of the department by the federal government. On March 24, 1989 an assistant U.S. attorney came to the station house in connection with the preparation of criminal charges against two police officers who had been indicted for possession and distribution of drugs. The officers had alleged that the grievant had participated with them in the use of cocaine.

It was not clear why the grievant came forward. The police department later explained that the meeting had been requested by the U.S. attorney, but, according to her, the grievant had unexpectedly asked for a meeting that day. His attorney also attended.

At the interview, the U.S. attorney told the grievant and his attorney that she could obtain a letter of limited immunity from the authorities in exchange for the grievant's testimony. The grievant was persuaded to tell his story. Among other matters, the grievant admitted using cocaine while in uniform on two occasions in 1983 and 1984, five years earlier. He snorted the cocaine once, and the other time he had tasted it.

When it turned out that immunity would not be forthcoming, the grievant refused to testify at the trial of the two officers, invoking Fifth Amendment rights. He was terminated by the police department.

At his subsequent arbitration, the grievant testified about the circumstances of his cocaine use, both times in the company of the officers on trial. After the second incident he had asked for a transfer, because he was afraid of what was going on and decided that it was dangerous to ride with those two officers.

The arbitrator, Tim Bornstein, had to decide whether or not the City had just cause to fire the grievant, and he decided that there were mitigating circumstances. He upheld the grievance, ordering the City to reinstate the grievant with full back pay.

Bornstein included the following statement in his award:

> We live in difficult times for law enforcement in America. Police, prosecutors and judges are under heavy pressure from the citizenry, elected officials, and the press to control the awful scourge of the illicit drug trade. Several presidents have declared war on the drug trade and drug use. In this war, law enforcement officials are on the front lines, and like all front line soldiers they are held to a high standard. However high that standard may be set, it must be fundamentally fair, not an impossible one.

Bornstein pointed out that the grievant's use of cocaine was reprehensible and inconsistent with his oath to uphold the law. It was also foolish. The grievant jeopardized his career, as well as his health and the welfare of his family, but the infractions, as wrong as they were, should be kept in perspective. The incidents took place five or six years before the department learned of them. There was no evidence that the grievant used cocaine on other occasions and no suggestion that he was an addict. In Bornstein's opinion, it was overly harsh to discharge an outstanding police officer for such an offense.

Based on the facts, one may share Bornstein's sympathy. The grievant was virtually trapped into a disclosure by the U.S. attorney who was unable to deliver on her promise of immunity.

A MATTER OF CREDIBILITY

Drug related cases often turn on the credibility of the witnesses. The people who report such incidents are often involved in the violation, and the question then becomes whether or not their testimony is credible.

Miami, Florida has become a notorious international drug center. The notorious Miami River Cops case revealed a scandalous example of police officers gone bad when a gang of police officers confiscated narcotics from illegal smugglers and sold them for a fortune.

Roger I. Abrams, Dean of Nova University Law School, was appointed to hear what he later said was the most remarkable arbitration he ever heard in his fourteen year career as an arbitrator.

During two days of hearings, Abrams listened to an extraordinary tale of police corruption told by three former Miami police officers, now convicted felons. According to these witnesses, the Miami police were involved in murders, armed robbery, and drug running. The three witnesses were flown to Miami from other parts of the country where they were living under new identities in the Federal Witness Protection Program. The hearings were guarded by a detachment of U.S. Marshalls.

The officers testifying against the grievant had been arrested on December 30, 1985, and they had been indicted, along with other Miami police officers, for conspiring to murder one of the government witnesses. The first criminal trial had ended after three and a half months with a mistrial.

The officers were indicted again on May 8, 1987 for the murder conspiracy. At that point the grievant decided to cooperate with the FBI. He had been fired for misconduct and accused of violating various regulations. At stake was his job and reputation, because the grievant claimed that the City had wrongfully discharged him.

The events surrounding the grievant's discharge occurred on July 12, 1985. According to the City, the grievant had asked a friend to sell cocaine. Furthermore, the grievant had been aware of a planned narcotics theft in which he had been invited to participate. He had failed to report the crime. The officer denied everything and testified that he had no knowledge of the theft, nor had he encouraged his friend to sell cocaine.

The government's witnesses testified that they had told the grievant about the upcoming theft, the so-called Tamiami Boatyard Rip-off, and they testified that he had received $800,000 as his share of the profits. The City based its case on the three witnesses, urging that they be believed and pointing out that they had nothing to gain from lying.

The union argued that the grievant should not have been discharged. The arbitrator should believe the grievant rather than convicted perjurers and drug traffickers. Also, the grievant voluntarily submitted to a polygraph, conducted by one of the nation's leading polygraphers, and the test corroborated the grievant's testimony.

Arbitrator Abrams first considered the admissibility of the polygraph test. The City argued that it should not be allowed into testimony, noting that polygraphs are notoriously unreliable. The union said the results of the test should be allowed. The arbitrator accepted the polygraph but only to corroborate other testimony.

The issue in this case was whether or not the officer had been discharged for just cause. Abrams said that he had tried to reconstruct the events based on the testimony, but there was no way to be sure exactly what had happened. Only the participants knew for certain, but the City had convinced him that the grievant had been involved in the criminal activities. He concluded that there was just cause to terminate the grievant.

This case turned on credibility. Should the arbitrator believe three convicted felons or the grievant who wanted his job back? Abrams believed the felons.

MUST AN OFFICER SUSPECTED OF DRUG USE TAKE A DRUG TEST?

An officer in Pomona, California was fired for refusing to take a drug test. The officer had been under surveillance because he frequented establishments where cocaine was sold and used. This led to a warrant to search his home where narcotic paraphernalia and a small amount of cocaine was found. On the following day, the officer was ordered to take a urine test after being told that the test was for administrative use only and that no charges would be lodged.

After talking to his lawyer, the officer refused to take the test. He was discharged for insubordination but filed a grievance.

Hearing officer William S. Rule had been arbitrating for twenty years. In his award, he concluded that "the grievant's refusal to take the test constituted insubordination, and was just cause for his termination if the order to take the test was lawful and proper." The entire case hinged on whether or not the order to provide a urine sample was appropriate.

The City argued that courts have generally supported the right to test police officers without a warrant, so long as there was reasonable suspicion of the use of drugs.

Rule found a flaw in the City's argument. The grievant was not working when he was ordered to submit to the test, because he had been placed on administrative leave so that his possible drug use could be investigated. Since he was not acting as a police officer, Rule concluded that the department had no need to determine whether or not he was using drugs. The City had admitted that the grievant had not been under the influence of drugs when his house was searched nor when he was ordered to take the test.

Arbitrator Rule upheld the grievance. "Fourth Amendment rights are important to individual freedom and must not be ignored without reasonable justification . . . Since the order to take the test without a warrant was unlawful under the circumstances of this case, the grievant may not be properly discharged for insubordination."

In similar situations most police investigators probably would have obtained a warrant. Then the illegal possession of cocaine would have been enough to justify the discharge or to require a test.

This case did not present a strong case for termination. Frequenting establishments where drugs are being sold is seldom considered to be a solid ground for discipline without some evidence of participation in the illicit activities.

TURNING FROM DRUGS TO ALCOHOL

The remaining cases in this chapter deal with alcohol abuse, which is probably as common among police officers as it is with average Americans. When drinking is combined with driving the combination can be lethal, particularly among the young males who make up the major part of many police forces.

The use of alcohol is widespread in the United States, and drinking often is encouraged. Alcoholism, the addiction to alcohol, is regarded as a medical problem rather than a crime, but when the abuse of alcohol interferes with an employee's work, most employers will encourage the worker to seek treatment. Arbitrators usually expect employers to provide rehabilitation to alcoholic employees before disciplining them.

An arbitrator will try to determine whether or not drinking has impaired an officer's job performance. Was the cop drunk on duty? Or did the drinking occur in private, becoming an employment problem only through absenteeism? Or poor performance? The interests of the public are carefully weighed as in other cases involving police officers. For example, off-duty drunkenness is sometimes the subject of departmental discipline, particularly driving under the influence. The next two cases involve grievants who were state troopers.

An Ohio state trooper with eleven months' seniority was arrested for drunken driving. His job had involved arresting motorists for exactly that crime, among other violations.

On July 28, 1989, while off-duty, he had consumed seven bottles of beer between 7:30 PM and midnight, and then went to bed. After midnight, a friend called him from Huntington, West Virginia and asked him to come over and give him a ride home, because the friend's car had broken down. The officer refused at first, but fifteen minutes later, his friend called again. This time the officer agreed to come for him.

While in Huntington the officer had two more beers while his friend and another man tried to fix the car. Finally, the three men drove back to Ohio in the officer's car. While driving along US Highway 52 near Ironton, Ohio at 6:30 in the morning, the officer ran off the highway. He damaged his car and smashed two highway guard rails. His friends tried to persuade him to leave the scene of the accident, but he refused to do so.

He flagged a motorist, asking him to report the accident to the state police. A few minutes later, a state trooper appeared at the scene. The officer told him what had happened and identified himself as a police officer, a fellow trooper. The state trooper smelled alcohol on his breath and arrested him. A test later showed that the officer's blood alcohol content was 0.18 percent. The superintendent placed the officer on administrative leave.

On August 21, the officer was charged with driving under the influence. He did not deny the charges and was sentenced to three days in jail with a $400 fine. After his conviction, he requested a transfer.

The media had a field day. In 1988, the Ohio State Highway Patrol had made 33,000 arrests for driving under the influence. Now, one of its troopers had been caught. His commanding officer received many phone calls complaining about the officer's behavior. People were saying that it tarnished the reputation of state police.

On September 7, the department terminated the grievant, on the basis that his conviction for driving under the influence was incompatible with his duty to meet a high standard of conduct both on- and off-duty.

The Fraternal Order of the Police acknowledged that the grievant should be punished but said that discharge was too harsh. In an earlier case, a female trooper had been arrested on similar charges and had been reinstated. The union emphasized the officer's integrity, shown by his decision to remain at the scene.

Arbitrator Calvin William Sharpe upheld the department's action, stating that termination was appropriate and justified by the contract. The State has "the right to expect that a professional standard of conduct be adhered to by all Highway Patrol personnel." The contract imposed a just cause standard of discipline for off-duty situations, and this case met that standard. Although the grievant's postaccident conduct reflected "some sensitivity to his ethical obligations," his driving drunk did not.

The arbitrator explained why the earlier case was not a precedent, because the female trooper had been acquitted by the court. This grievant's conviction justified the action taken by the State. Sharpe denied the grievance by applying the usual standards applied by arbitrators in such cases:

- Did the grievant's behavior harm the reputation of the employer?
- Did the behavior render the employee unable to perform the assigned duties?

- Did the behavior lead other employees to refuse or be reluctant to work with the employee?

In this case, the arbitrator answered all three in the affirmative.

A SIMILAR CASE BUT AN OPPOSITE DECISION

Soon afterward, another Ohio arbitrator came to an opposite conclusion in a strikingly similar case. Again, the facts were not on dispute. The officer had been working for two years as a highway patrol trooper. On September 1990, he was on the midnight to 8 AM shift. After work, he spent the day playing golf and drinking beer with a buddy. He admitted to drinking about eight beers. Shortly after 4 PM his buddy dropped him off at his parent's home. Afterwards, the officer went to another friend's house, where he took a nap. After waking up, he called the station and told the dispatcher that he had the flu. That evening, he went with a friend to a bar and drank a six pack of beer in less than three hours. While at the bar, he ran into his cousin. At about 2:30 AM, the three men went back to his friend's house. Soon afterwards, the officer agreed to drive his cousin home.

A local police officer from the town of Mount Vernon noticed a car being driven erratically. The driver seemed to be drunk, because the car was swerving all over the road and riding up on the shoulder. It barely missed a parked car. She pulled the car over. When she asked the driver for his license, he showed her his trooper identification. He performed the heel-to-toe test awkwardly and had trouble keeping his balance. She placed him under arrest. He agreed to a blood alcohol test that rated him at 0.18 percent, twice the legal limit.

The officer subsequently pleaded guilty, was fined $350, served five days in jail, and had his driver's license suspended for ninety days. He was terminated by the Highway Patrol for violating departmental rules, but a grievance was filed on his behalf by the Fraternal Order of Police.

In this case, the arbitrator decided that discharge was too harsh a penalty. Progressive discipline would have been more appropriate. According to the arbitrator, Patricia Bittel of Cleveland, the State should have considered "the circumstances of the alcohol use, the opportunities, if any, given for rehabilitation, the likelihood the individual will benefit from treatment and the factual background of the case."

The collective bargaining contract provided that employees would receive help in locating treatment for their alcoholism but that this was not intended to waive other provisions. A just cause provision was part of the contract. This was the issue. Was the grievant terminated for just cause?

In the course of her testimony, the arresting officer testified that she would have difficulty working with an officer who had been arrested for drunken driving, but so far as she knew, the grievant's cousin was the only one, other than herself, who knew about the case. There had been no publicity.

The grievant's lieutenant testified that the various cases on which the grievant had been the arresting officer would now have to be dropped since the grievant could no longer be a credible witness. The lieutenant also pointed out that the officer's abuse of sick leave was also a violation of departmental rules. A captain of the highway patrol also testified, and he said that the Toledo Blade was preparing an article about excessive drinking among state troopers.

In his defense the grievant said that he had never called in sick before and that this was the first time that alcohol had interfered with his work. He had served three days in jail and had not taken a drink since.

According to the arbitrator, the grievant's participation in rehabilitation should have been a mitigating factor. She was impressed by the fact that the grievant had avoided alcohol since the incident, that he had severed relationships with his drinking friends, and had pursued a program of rehabilitation "with variable progress but no regression." As she pointed out, he was not an "alcoholic," merely an "abuser."

These two cases involving Ohio state troopers are remarkably similar. Both involve young, relatively junior officers, neither of whom was yet a confirmed alcoholic. Both troopers made drunk driving arrests as part of their job, and, when tested, their blood alcohol was almost identical.

The amount of publicity may have played a part in the arbitrators' decisions, particularly in the case heard by Sharpe. He confirmed the discharge, while arbitrator Bittel upheld the grievance. Perhaps these decisions merely illustrate that with essentially the same facts, arbitrators can come to different conclusions.

The major difference between the cases seemed to be whether or not the incident was publicized in the local press, a factor that some arbitrators might deem to be irrelevant.

A CONTRASTING CASE FROM TEXAS

A case in Austin, Texas offers an interesting contrast. A police officer with a record of alcoholism and other infractions spent a holiday with his children by his former wife and his present wife's brothers in the nearby town of Elgin where they lived. On January 24, 1988 he drank several glasses of wine at a family party. At about 6 o'clock, he returned his children to his ex-wife's home, and on the way back to the party, he bought another bottle of wine. He and his wife, a fellow Austin police officer, got into a heated argument soon after he returned, after which she drove home. He decided to spend the night at another officer's home. By now, it was almost ten o'clock.

While driving on Highway 1704, the officer lost control of his car, went off the road, then skidded back across the highway through a wire fence, across a dirt road, rolled over four or five times, and finally came to rest 200 feet from where the car left the highway. Skid marks indicated that he crossed the highway at sixty-seven miles per hour, which indicated that he was going even faster when he first left the highway.

Having escaped serious injury, he began to walk back the way he came, passing several occupied houses. Finally, after walking half a mile, he stopped at a house and called his wife, who agreed to come for him. Witnesses at the house later testified that he was wearing blue jeans and a pullover and was bleeding from a scratch on his back.

Elgin medical service technicians arrived at the scene of the accident at about quarter after ten. They found no one in the car but discovered the officer's service revolver on the ground, next to an open bottle with some wine left in it.

The officer and his wife passed the scene of the accident on the way home but did not stop. Their phone was ringing when they arrived home. It was the Elgin police. His wife was asked to bring the grievant's license and insurance papers to the scene of the accident. She did so but asked the medical technicians to follow her home because she was worried that her husband might have been seriously injured. They later testified that, when they saw him, the officer's eyes were bloodshot and his speech was slurred. A state trooper who came with them thought the grievant was intoxicated but only charged him with speeding.

The officer did not report the accident to his superiors but called his sergeant to say that he would not come to work in the morning. On the following day, he was treated for muscular strains to his back and neck, but x-rays showed no permanent damage.

One month later, after an investigation, the officer was placed on restricted status and later put on indefinite suspension, tantamount to termination. During the investigation, he had been asked to sign a release for his medical records. After signing, he had second thoughts and instructed the hospital not to release the information. He filed a grievance.

Arbitrator Ernest E. Marlatt had been arbitrating for almost twenty years. After a full hearing, at which the officer was represented by two attorneys, Marlatt denied the grievance. The City had charged the grievant with three acts of misconduct. The arbitrator determined that two of the three grounds were valid, which justified the suspension. Marlatt found that the officer had been intoxicated. The EMS paramedics, who were trained in identifying that condition, testified that he was drunk when they saw him that evening, and the nearly empty bottle of wine found at the accident corroborated their testimony. The grievant's history of alcohol abuse, his avoidance of contact with residents near the scene, and his refusal to go to the hospital for examination all supported the inference that he was intoxicated and made a calculated effort to avoid discovery.

If he had not been drunk, there would have been no reason to cover up. An off-duty accident would have been a relatively minor infraction. No one was hurt. The news media did not report the accident. Certainly, the officer's conduct had not been so bad that other officers would have refused to work with him.

The second charge involved interfering with the investigation. The grievant had refused to cooperate with the internal affairs division or to produce his medical records. According to Marlatt, "The fact that the grievant was capable of making such a colossal error in judgment is itself evidence that he should not be sent back on the streets with a badge and deadly weapon."

The City failed to prove the third charge, that the officer made a false statement when asked whether or not he had changed his clothing between the time of the accident and when the EMS vehicle arrived at his home, but this was not essential to the City's case.

A unique aspect of the arbitrator's decision was that he independently questioned the constitutionality of a statute under which the grievant was charged, that police officers must obey laws of the United States, Texas, and the City of Austin. He pointed out that such a statute covered thousands of laws and regulations that had no criminal sanctions and no specific relationship to employment, but, Marlatt continued, the grievant's "experienced counsel" had failed to raise that issue.

In this case, there was nothing to mitigate the disciplinary action or to suggest that the grievant be given another chance. His record was deplorable, exhibiting a chronic problem with alcohol. All of the grievant's supervisors agreed that he had been an embarrassment to the department.

According to the arbitrator, the officer's deliberate attempt to conceal the facts was particularly reprehensible. As a police officer, the grievant should have cooperated with the investigation. If the grievant had admitted at the time of the accident that he was drunk, he probably would have received no more than a fifteen day suspension.

"It is the grievant's demonstrated lack of responsibility and integrity, not his drunk driving, which justifies the chief's determination that the grievant is unfit to serve honorably as a law enforcement officer."

EVEN A GOOD RECORD MAY BE NO DEFENSE

In another case involving a San Antonio policeman, the grievant during his three years as a police officer had an excellent record. One morning in February, he was apprehended while driving off-duty. When pulled over, he had been speeding and driving erratically.

The arresting officer gave the grievant a blood alcohol test. He scored 0.16 percent. The State of Texas considers 0.10 percent proof of intoxication. On that basis, he was convicted of driving while intoxicated and was terminated by the police department. The officer admitted his mistake, but filed a grievance on the basis that discharge was too harsh a penalty, particularly since he had been off-duty.

The City's position was that any officer convicted of such a crime should not be allowed to continue on the force, because it would be detrimental to the department and would undermine the public trust.

Arbitrator Tim Bornstein from Boston was reluctant to sustain a discharge for off-duty infractions, because what people do on their own time is their own business; however, police officers are subject to higher standards than other employees. "In an isolated instance of off-duty intoxication for most workers, there is little or no relationship to individual ability to perform his job," Bornstein wrote. However, he pointed out that in San Antonio drinking is a major problem, particularly where public safety is involved. Also, the City sometimes requires police officers to work on short notice.

The grievant should have known of the public's heightened concern about drunk driving, and the primary responsibility of the police force is to protect the public.

A single incident of drunk driving may not threaten the efficiency of the department, Bornstein said, but when an officer commits a serious breach of the law that he is entrusted to enforce, it reflects on the department. It is the responsibility of the chief to take whatever steps are required to ensure that the public has confidence in the department. That trust is critical. In the absence of proof that the chief of police had acted arbitrarily or capriciously, Bornstein refused to substitute his judgment for that of the department. He denied the grievance.

SUMMARY

As the arbitration decisions in this chapter indicate, the use of drugs and alcohol by police officers, even when they are off-duty, can be hazardous to their employment. Police are held to a higher standard than are other employees. If their substance abuse prejudices their ability to serve or hurts the reputation of their department, they are likely to be terminated and have their punishment upheld by an arbitrator.

There are exceptions. Individual arbitrators may be swayed by mitigating factors, such as an exemplary record. Nevertheless, a police officer is expected to behave. Drunk driving or taking drugs, even while off-duty, is likely to be punished. As one arbitrator put it, it comes with the badge.

CHAPTER 7

Other Off-Duty Offenses

For most employees, job responsibilities end when they leave work. What they do then is their own affair. Even if they commit a crime, so long as they are not incarcerated or incapacitated, they are free to come to work on the following morning. Police officers do not have that luxury. They carry the reputation of their department with them, even when they are off-duty, and cops are frequently disciplined for off-duty conduct.

What if an officer has a fight while off-duty? Should a cop be penalized for punching his girlfriend? If she files a complaint, should he be punished? Some departments think so. In one of the cases described in this chapter, exactly that issue was arbitrated and decided.

On the other hand, an officer with a long, good service record should not be discharged for one minor infraction. One such mistake should not destroy an officer's career; however, police officers are held to high standards by labor arbitrators, because the police are expected to protect the public. If an officer does something that shows that such confidence is misplaced, the police department can be expected to respond. A police department cannot have its reputation tarnished by a bad cop.

In the following cases, officers were disciplined for off-duty activities. In some of these cases, the department's judgment is upheld by an arbitrator, while in others, it is not.

A CASE OF OFF-DUTY VIOLENCE

Some police officers are violent, and when that violence takes place off-duty, it may be treated as grounds for discipline. Such a situation arose in Pasadena, Texas where a police officer with five years' seniority was suspended for three off-duty incidents.

On January 24, he was involved in a fight with his girlfriend in the middle of the night in his apartment. The police came after a neighbor complained that the noise was disturbing the neighborhood. When they arrived, the officer was bleeding from a scratch on his face, and the girlfriend said that he had threatened her with his gun.

In February, the officer abused the same woman in a public parking lot in Houston. As she tried to walk away from him, he pulled her back by her hair, and she almost fell. As he pushed her into his car, she was crying.

In March, the police again responded when the woman was heard screaming in the officer's apartment. This incident finally prompted an investigation. Afterwards the City indefinitely suspended the officer on the ground that his behavior was unbecoming as an officer. The officer denied all of the charges and initiated an arbitration.

Texas law states that "disgraceful conduct" or "conduct unbecoming an officer" justifies termination. The department alleged that the grievant's off-duty behavior met those criteria.

The grievant's attorney admitted that strict standards were appropriate for police officers but said that none of the incidents justified the action taken by the City. The incidents occurred while the officer was off-duty and were between consenting adults. They did not prejudice the officer's ability to perform his duties.

Arbitrator Diane Dunham Massey was skeptical. In a lengthy opinion, she reviewed the evidence. She found it difficult to credit the testimony of either the grievant or his girlfriend, but several independent witnesses had confirmed the facts. She pointed out that police officers do not enjoy the privacy of ordinary people. Here, the grievant's violent activities "bled over into the public perception. Too many citizens were observing what they described as startling, inappropriate behavior . . . a strong possibility that the grievant was not always in full control of his emotions." Police officers "must not only have a stable emotional makeup," they must also display such stability at all times to avoid the implication that they are not suited for their job. Massey said that a police department cannot employ people who appear violent or unstable. Someone who explodes in domestic situations may not have a problem on the job, she said, but the grievant's constant fights with his girlfriend cast a long shadow on his ability to perform as a police officer. Also, the grievant had earlier incidents of misbehavior on his record, including one where he shot himself. This too convinced the arbitrator that the grievance should be denied.

Most people would agree with the arbitrator that people who are constantly beating up their girlfriends are not appropriate candidates for long-term employment as police officers.

ANOTHER VIOLENT POLICE OFFICER

A Fort Lauderdale case also tested the on-duty behavior of a police officer but concerned a purely personal relationship. The officer's girlfriend came looking for him, and he punched her in the face.

On April 26, 1988, at about 11:00 PM, another officer was in the precinct parking lot putting equipment into his patrol car when he heard a woman screaming in a nearby parking lot. Investigating, he found that she was shouting at a friend of his, a fellow officer, who was off-duty and who assured him that it was only an argument and asked him to help get rid of the woman. The officer asked her to leave. After yelling some more, she got into a nearby car and was driven away. The woman had been the fellow officer's girlfriend for over a year and a half and had occasionally shared her apartment with that officer.

Later that evening, the officer was on patrol in the girlfriend's neighborhood, and she came over to talk to him. The officer asked her about her swollen and discolored left cheek, and the woman told him that she had asked his fellow officer to return the key to her apartment, and they had had an argument. Afterwards, she said that he had followed her in his patrol car. During a later argument, he grabbed her by the hair and hit her. She said that he had threatened to kill her if she told anyone.

The officer informed his supervisor of that conversation. Several days later, the supervisor sent a memo to the district commander reporting the incident, and Internal Affairs started an investigation. The girlfriend considered filing charges but decided against it.

There was another witness to the incident, and this was the driver of the car in which the girlfriend had been riding. When Internal Affairs interviewed her, the woman said that the officer grabbed his girlfriend by her pony-tail and yanked her toward the window, then the officer had hit her in the eye. This incident took place while the officer was on-duty.

On June 15, the department informed the officer that he was suspended without pay from June 18 to July 12, at which time he would be terminated.

The union filed a grievance, pointing out that the employer had the burden of proof. The girlfriend had been the aggressor, because she had sought out the grievant as he had begun his duties. According to the union, there was no proof that the grievant ever struck the woman. His girlfriend had refused to say that he had hit her and denied it under oath. The union pointed out that the grievant had just one prior reprimand in his record and that had been challenged. He should, therefore, be given the benefit of the doubt, and the penalty should at least be reduced. Because the girlfriend could not control her temper was no reason to discipline the grievant.

The City introduced two disinterested witnesses who described the fight. Neither had any reason to lie. They said that the officer had assaulted the woman in full public view.

William L. Richard had been a full-time arbitrator since 1982. He pointed out that everyone agreed that the grievant and his girlfriend had engaged in a public argument. Nor was it in dispute that she had told the original officer that the grievant had hit her. The arbitrator was convinced that the girl was a liar. But was she lying when she said that the grievant hit her? Or was she lying when she said that it had never happened? The arbitrator felt that the other witnesses were more reliable because they had nothing to gain. The arbitrator decided that the City had just cause for discharging the officer, because his conduct was "unbecoming an officer."

In this case the fight occurred while the grievant was on-duty, but the relationship was primarily an off-duty affair. Would the result have been any different if the fight had taken place during the officer's off hours?

EVEN MORE BIZARRE BEHAVIOR

Another off-duty case involved a somewhat more unusual situation. In El Paso, Texas, on Halloween night, October 31, 1987, a female patrol officer decided to take her roommate to a Halloween costume party at "Our Memories," a lesbian bar in a shabby part of town. She supposedly wore a Keystone Kops helmet and a pig snout mask over her police service uniform, including badge, night stick, pistol belt, and service revolver. A witness later testified that she had live ammunition in her belt.

Her roommate wore a motorcycle costume, consisting of black leather boots, a torn T-shirt, a collar with silver studs, and fake tattoos. They entered the bar handcuffed together at about 10:30 PM. Seventy-five other guests were already there, and one of the patrons asked the officer if she was a real cop.

"What's it to you?" the officer responded, "I can do anything I want."

Although the officer later denied it, she was also observed drinking a bottle of beer. The officer and her roommate left the party at midnight. One of the patrons, an ex-convict with no love for police officers, decided to file a complaint.

A sergeant from Internal Affairs investigated the incident. The officer denied that she wore her police uniform or took a weapon to the bar, and she denied that she had been drinking. According to her, both she and her roommate wore identical motorcycle outfits. After interviewing other witnesses, the sergeant was convinced that the officer's statement was false. At a second interview, she admitted that she had worn her uniform but still denied drinking alcohol that evening.

The City charged the officer with discrediting the department, and she was terminated. At a subsequent arbitration hearing, she was represented by an attorney from the Municipal Police Officers Association. Arbitrator Marlatt, who was selected for the case, showed little sympathy for the grievant.

According to him, her actions were not simply poor judgment, but showed disrespect for her uniform. By lying about the incident, the grievant made it even worse, because she acknowledged that her misconduct was more than an error in judgment. Otherwise, she would have admitted the facts.

The arbitrator denied the grievance. The City had just cause to fire the grievant, because the police department deserves loyalty from every officer on the force. Cops have the right of free speech and free expression like other citizens, but they do not have the right to ridicule fellow officers by debasing their uniform as a ludicrous Halloween costume. In the opinion of the arbitrator, termination was warranted.

The grievant in this case may have miscalculated, thinking that in the counterculture society that frequents lesbian bars she would be free from her police obligations. She was wrong, but how could she know that an ex-con would report her to the department?

SHOPLIFTING AS AN OFF-DUTY OFFENSE

Dr. Michael Marmo of Xavier University in Cincinnati, an authority on the police, published a report on police grievances in the *Journal of Police Science and Administration* in 1986. Marmo concluded that administrators should have the right to discipline police officers for any off-duty behavior that had an adverse impact on their department. Arbitrators generally support that view. Because of the susceptibility of police departments to adverse publicity, police are held to higher standards of off-duty behavior than workers in other types of employment. Marmo found it difficult, however, to forecast exactly what standard an arbitrator would apply when determining whether or not a particular behavior had an adverse impact upon the department.

He reported a case where a deputy sheriff was terminated for shoplifting two packages of mens' underwear from a supermarket while off-duty. The arbitrator converted the discharge to a four month suspension based on the grievant's excellent previous record. The grievant had been "a fine, even exemplary deputy sheriff, earning the plaudits of his chief, superiors and fellow deputies."

What follows are other cases where police officers were caught shoplifting. Shoplifting is a fairly common crime, and it is indulged in by at least a few police officers. When they are caught and the department punishes them, sympathy may be aroused because of the pettiness of the crime, compared to the harsh penalty of prejudicing a chosen career.

A Philadelphia police officer with eighteen years of good conduct took a cassette case from a Best Store in Tredyffrin Township on December 22, 1988. In the parking lot, he was apprehended by a local cop who braced him against the wall and asked for his wallet. The off-duty officer ran away and hid. Back-up police were called for. One and a half hours later, the officer surrendered and was taken to the local police station—a sad story.

There was no dispute about the incident. The officer was suspended from employment pending a criminal action by the Philadelphia police department, but a grievance was filed on his behalf by the Fraternal Order of Police.

At the arbitration, the City argued that shoplifting was conduct unbecoming an officer and, if not punished, would destroy public confidence in the department. The grievant not only took merchandise from the store, but he also resisted arrest and fled the scene.

The union defended the grievant on the basis of his mental condition. He had been suffering from psychological problems for which he had recently completed a rehabilitation program. The City should reinstate the grievant as it had reinstated other officers after successful rehabilitation, because the officer had harmed only himself.

Arbitrator Walter H. Powell agreed that the officer had been acting under stress, and may not have been fully responsible for his actions. He had been diagnosed as having suffered "a mental breakdown due to pressures and stress of his job and personal obligations which he felt had to be fulfilled." The criminal court had ordered the grievant to participate in a rehabilitation program, and the officer had complied with the court order and was continuing to work with a psychologist. On that basis, the court had dropped the criminal charges.

The arbitrator noted that the police department had not been consistent in dealing with similar offenses. The differences in the facts of such cases had not been enough to justify such disparate treatment. The arbitrator concluded that a single incident should not destroy eighteen years of exemplary service. The grievant had been "an excellent policeman who gave fully of himself to his duties." The arbitrator reinstated the grievant but without back pay for the three years that the matter had been pending.

It is unusual for a labor arbitration to be decided so long after the incident, because most cases are concluded a few months after being filed for arbitration. In this situation, the parties probably agreed to defer the hearings until the criminal action and the subsequent rehabilitation were completed. Since the arbitrator did not reimburse the grievant for lost back pay, the penalty in this case to the grievant was severe. On the other hand, during his suspension the grievant had found employment, according to the arbitrator's opinion.

ANOTHER CASE OF SHOPLIFTING

Another Philadelphia police officer offered a different justification for his shoplifting. On May 5, 1988, on his day off, the officer walked out of a Clover Department Store with some drill bits in his hand and two bottles of cologne in his pocket, which he had not paid for. When outside, he was confronted by two store detectives, who wrestled him to the ground. Then he was taken to the store's security office.

When arrested, the officer became ill and was taken to Nazareth Hospital, where he was kept for observation for a heart condition for a week. While he was in the hospital, he was charged with theft and suspended by his department.

The discharging physician reported that the officer had been taking over one hundred amino acid and vitamin pills each day. The officer ranked twenty-seventh in the nation as an amateur power lifter but reportedly was having anxiety attacks during sex and in other stressful situations. The attacks involved sharp chest pains and a feeling of disorientation.

At the arbitration hearing, the issue was whether the grievant had intended to take the articles without paying or was suffering from an anxiety condition that made him rush out of the building. His physician testified that he did not believe that the grievant had intended to steal the items. The officer was suffering from a severe anxiety attack, so that when he left the store, he was seeking fresh air to help relieve his symptoms. The hospital psychiatrist confirmed the doctor's theory, explaining that the patient was close to tears as he told about the incident and described the stress he was suffering at work.

"I can only sleep two hours a night—I was crying in the locker room—I didn't want to go to work because I was barraged with orders, pushed here and there, and asked to take on more accountability."

The City's medical director recommended that the grievant be returned to active duty, but the City's review board could not decide whether the grievant left the store because of a panic attack or whether the panic attack was a result of being arrested. The City's position, however, was that the grievant's conduct was unbecoming an officer, no matter what the cause.

The Fraternal Order of Police argued that the grievant was being victimized. He had always wanted to be a "perfect cop," and he had received over thirty commendations for bravery, heroism, and merit. He had demonstrated his honesty by refusing substantial bribes, up to $50,000. According to the union the word of two store detectives should not be accepted over that of a superior police officer. The medical director's recommendation should not have been dismissed.

Arbitrator Kinnard Lang had to decide why the grievant left the store. He studied 500 pages of transcript, as well as videotapes taken by the store. Did the grievant leave the store as a petty thief or because of his panic attack?

In deciding the case, Lang considered the grievant's personality. His courage and honesty had been tested in the line of duty, and he had been promoted to sergeant and given responsibility for supervising a group of rookie cops. Lang concluded that the officer was not a petty thief. The more likely explanation was that he left the store to get fresh air to relieve his panic attack. The panic attack had been caused by the stress of his recent promotion, and his new role as stepfather to his fiancée's twelve-year-old son.

The arbitrator believed that the officer was not without some responsibility, but the City did not have just cause to terminate him. Nevertheless, he should have sought medical help sooner. The arbitrator ordered the grievant to be reinstated but without back pay. His absence from work while the case was pending should be treated as an unpaid medical leave.

STILL ANOTHER SHOPLIFTING CASE

Shoplifting can also become part of a person's life-style, rather than an occasional escapade. An example of this occurred in Austin, Texas and involved a senior police officer.

On November 17, 1989, the officer stole certain items worth about $200 from Foley's Department Store. Additional merchandise was found in the trunk of his car. The employees at the store said that the grievant had acted like a professional shoplifter, not like an amateur. The security officer had to put handcuffs on him to get him back into the store.

The officer admitted to shoplifting, but said that his actions were involuntary. He showed no remorse. He said he was undergoing a difficult time in his life, because his father had been arrested for indecency with his own granddaughter, his brother had been arrested for burglary, and he was having marital problems. Shoplifting was his cry for help.

Unfortunately, his psychologist did not support that theory. He testified that his patient was suffering from depression but that this would not account for shoplifting.

In criminal court, he pleaded *nolo contendere*. On March 30, 1990 he received an indefinite suspension. The City claimed that the officer's actions brought discredit upon the department, negating his effectiveness as an officer of the law.

The arbitrator, Professor Elvis C. Stephens, was asked to decide whether or not the City had just cause to terminate the grievant. The items the grievant stole were not small trinkets. Some of them he could use, such as neck ties and dress shirts, while others could have been returned for store credit, as the grievant had done before with items he had stolen.

A police department psychologist said that the grievant seemed to like living on the edge. From the description of his behavior, the psychologist concluded that shoplifting was not a cry for help but a test of his ability to avoid being caught. He enjoyed the excitement.

Some fellow officers said that the grievant was a capable officer, but his ex-partner testified that he would no longer be able to work with him.

Professor Stephens decided that the City had proved its case, that the penalty was proper. The grievant's shoplifting was a pattern of behavior that met the grievant's need to take chances and to put himself in stressful situations. If anything, the job stress that he encountered in his assignments on the Hispanic crime unit probably helped to satisfy the same need for excitement.

Shoplifting, like other forms of criminal activity, may signal psychological problems or it may be a chronic behavioral pattern that is inconsistent with service as a police officer. The issue for the arbitrator is not whether the grievant should be salvaged or terminated. The question is whether or not the department has just cause to terminate the grievant for his behavior.

OTHER OFF-DUTY CONDUCT LEADING TO DISCIPLINE

Sometimes off-duty behavioral violations are combined with alcohol abuse, but the discipline is imposed for the behavior, not the drunkenness. Professor Marmo cited such a case in the article cited earlier. Three police officers borrowed a police cruiser during an off-duty drinking spree and drove 200 miles to visit some women. They were discharged. The police department asserted a "right to require its officers to conform their behavior to higher standards of conduct than may be required of non-public employees." The arbitrator dismissed their subsequent grievance. The use of the cruiser was an important part of the case against them.

The theory is that police must show respect for the law to earn credibility with people who might be inclined to break the law. Society expects lawbreakers to be captured, convicted, and sentenced for their actions, and it expects police officers to be law abiding. When officers break the law and are punished, arbitrators generally uphold the discipline imposed by the department.

Even when a violation seems trivial, an arbitrator is likely to support departmental discipline. An officer was suspended for a few days for not wearing his uniform hat while acting as a security officer at a health center while working off-duty. An arbitrator agreed that the officer should conform to the rules. He "occupies a position in which his status as a police officer is the governing factor." The uniform identifies him to the public as a police officer. When an officer is in uniform, the public rightfully assumes that he is enforcing the law on behalf of the City. He represents the police department, therefore, he must abide by departmental dress codes.

Off-duty activities are also carried out in civilian clothes. In another case cited by Dr. Marmo, an officer was terminated after a fight with another man over a woman. The department claimed that the incident was prejudicial to its reputation. Here, the arbitrator did not agree, pointing out that "it would be shocking to assume that the reputation and good name of the department are held hostage to the irresponsible vaporings of a spiteful boyfriend, beclouded by drink, whose vision of events is basically implausible."

THE IMPORTANCE OF IMAGE

Where culprits are identified in the press as being police officers, disciplining action may follow. Dr. Marmo cited a case where over a hundred people were arrested in a raid on an illegal gambling operation. A few police officials were among them. They, of course, were featured in the newspaper, and they were disciplined.

Police officers do not entirely lose their rights to privacy, but there are restrictions on those rights. Dr. Marmo described another case where a police officer, who was also president of his union, published a letter in a local newspaper, criticizing the department. The City claimed that he had violated a regulation requiring such material to be approved in advance by the police chief. The union argued that the rule did not apply because the letter was written on its behalf and, in any case, such censorship would have violated the grievant's constitutional rights.

The arbitrator agreed that it would cripple the union's right to engage in collective bargaining to have to obtain prior approval of such material, even though some articles might be "irresponsible or damaging to the proper functioning of the police bureau," which was not the case in this situation.

The arbitrator refused to rule on the grievant's constitutional rights, saying that such questions should be decided by the courts, not by an arbitrator.

It is common for contracts to state that police officers must conduct themselves at all times in a manner that is above reproach, so as "to reflect credit on the department," or "to avoid bringing discredit on themselves or the department." Dr. Marmo explains that such provisions are an attempt to require the officer's off-duty behavior to reflect well on the department. When an officer violates the criminal law, the department will claim that such a provision has been violated. The question is where to draw the line.

If the contract identifies specific behavior that will subject an officer to discipline, a more exact standard is applicable. Certain activities may be prohibited, such as working as an ambulance driver, serving as a volunteer fireman, employment in unsavory enterprises, all of which have been specified in contracts and have been upheld by arbitrators. The concept is well understood, but its application is sometimes difficult.

An arbitrator may have to be convinced that such a rule is reasonably related to an officer's fitness and capacity to serve. Evansville, Indiana passed a regulation that prohibited police officers from working where alcoholic beverages were bought or consumed. The Fraternal Order of Police filed a lawsuit to have the regulation declared invalid. The chief of police argued that while working in a bar an officer might overlook criminal activities to maximize business. The court was not impressed and invalidated the regulation, but similar restrictions on part-time employment of police officers are relatively common in many other jurisdictions.

RECKLESS DRIVING RESULTS IN DEATH

The primary notion in these cases is that an off-duty infraction by the officer must be job-related. One more case makes that point. On May 1, 1986 a Philadelphia police officer was involved in a car crash while off-duty. He was charged with two counts of involuntary manslaughter and two counts of vehicular homicide, convicted and sentenced to 10 years of probation, 2,000 hours of community service, and a $2,500 fine.

The officer had worked for the City since 1982 and had never been disciplined prior to the accident. Nevertheless, he was fired from his position as an evidence technician.

The grievant's union, AFSCME (Local 1637) filed a demand for arbitration. The union acknowledged that the City had the right to discipline employees for criminal conduct, but the crime must relate to the employment. The grievant argued that the accident had nothing to do with his employment and that his excellent job record showed his commitment to his job.

Arbitrator A. Martin Herring was asked to decide whether or not the City had just cause to terminate the grievant.

The City argued that, as a result of the grievant's criminal record, he could no longer testify in criminal prosecutions. An evidence technician's criminal record might be brought out by defense lawyers to challenge the credibility of the technician's testimony.

The arbitrator was not convinced that such a conviction would inhibit the grievant's performance. The grievant could still testify and stand the scrutiny of cross-examination. Herring pointed out that no evidence technician is perfect as to either education or credentials. The grievant's criminal record would not create an impossible barrier because his crime was not perjury or otherwise related to credibility. Accordingly, the arbitrator reinstated the grievant. He ordered the City to compensate the grievant with back pay and to reinstate his seniority.

SUMMARY

More so than in other occupations, a police officer's off-duty derelictions are thought to reflect upon his work. The cop who assaults a spouse, the shoplifter, and the officer convicted of a crime may be disciplined when the facts are known. Thus, to some extent, a police officer is never entirely off-duty and is always a representative of the police department. For some officers, this may contribute some measure of additional stress.

CHAPTER 8

Violating Departmental Policies

Every police department has rules that officers are obliged to follow. Indeed, police officers may have to observe more rules than most workers, but there are many reasons for this, including that police officers work under civil service regulations, police departments are authoritarian organizations that feast on regulations, and the working life of a police officer is filled with unanticipated challenges. They are expected to direct traffic, rescue kittens from high places, engage in car chases, and intervene in domestic disputes—all in one day. No wonder that rules and regulations proliferate.

In addition to detailed regulations about wearing a uniform, maintaining a service revolver, and filing numerous reports, a police officer is expected to be zealous, brave, and honest while avoiding behavior that might be considered "unbecoming an officer," the final fall-back rule. Some rules are unduly trivial. To be disciplined for not getting a haircut makes a police officer's career particularly frustrating, but the files contain grievance arbitration awards dealing with the proper length of hair, sideburns, mustaches, and beards, in addition to all of the minutiae of wearing a proper uniform.

In my community, for example, the police took to growing beards as a way of expressing displeasure with the town's bargaining position, and a grievance was filed to resolve the dispute. This case is included because it illustrates the kinds of problems that seem to occur most frequently in organizations where employees operate under a blanket of rules and regulations. Such an atmosphere can cause additional stress when combined with normal duties. In addition to worrying about armed criminals, police officers have to worry about trivia, such as whether or not their hair is hanging over their ears.

THE CASE OF THE UNRULY HAIR

The Hamilton County Sheriff's Department in Cincinnati trimmed its definition of hair grooming in early 1988. One detective, a man with twenty-two years of service, refused to comply. Prior to that date, the sheriff's department had required all male personnel to have a neat, tapered haircut, so as not to appear disheveled. Under that regulation, there had been no problems.

When the controversy actually began in 1987, the sheriff formed a committee to review departmental policies. One subcommittee investigated the grooming standards of the Cincinnati police department and the state highway patrol and recommended changes in the sheriff's haircut rule. The new rule said that "in no case shall the hair on the side of the head be of such length that it exceeds a line perpendicular to the top of the ear." The new rule went into effect on January 1, 1988.

Soon after the new rule took effect, the detective already mentioned was warned, then received two formal notices of noncompliance and a direct order to comply. Finally, he was told that discipline was being recommended, and in March, he was given a five day suspension.

The officer believed that suspension was too severe a punishment, and his union, the Fraternal Order of Police, filed a grievance. When he appeared at the arbitration hearing, the grievant's hair still hung down over his ears.

The City described the many times the grievant had been ordered to cut his hair, because it was not in conformance with the rule. His refusal to comply, according to the City, amounted to insubordination.

The grievant had unusually small ears, which sat close to his head. The union pointed out that if the grievant cut his hair in a line perpendicular to the top of his ear, "his barber would have had to shave him bald on the sides." It accused the sheriff of "splitting hairs" and punishing the grievant for a minor deviation.

Arbitrator Patricia Thomas Bittel was skeptical. She pointed out that the City had a legitimate need for officers to be neat in public and to foster discipline and esprit de corps.

The grievant said that he would lose his identity if he complied with the new rule, but her opinion was that the rule intended to accomplish exactly that, a loss of individualism in favor of a uniform identity.

The record indicated that no other employee had complained about the new regulation and that the City had initially treated the infraction as a minor offense, simply reminding the grievant that he needed a haircut. His repeated and deliberate refusal to get a haircut, however, changed the nature of the violation and it became insubordination, particularly after a direct order had been given. The arbitrator found that the employer had just cause to impose a five day suspension.

One wonders why the participants in this arbitration felt it necessary to go through such an elaborate adversarial process to determine whether or not this officer could be punished for allowing his hair to grow over his ears. Would any private sector employer allow itself to be seduced into squabbling over such a trivial issue?

The grievant had been the subject of other such confrontations during his long years of service, but was arbitration the best way to deal with such an attitude problem? Was the grievant suffering from a compulsive identity crisis? Was this an appropriate use of arbitration?

CONDUCT UNBECOMING AN OFFICER

Police officers are human, and like other workers, they sometimes break the rules. Sometimes they tell lies, are disrespectful, take what is not theirs, and use their position to their own advantage. This is wrong. When cops misbehave, they should be punished, and when police officers are untrustworthy, they may not be in the right profession. Society needs to be able to trust its police officers.

In most American communities, police have a solid reputation, but there are exceptions: There are bad police departments, bad precincts, and bad individual officers. In order to guard against such situations, most collective bargaining contracts contain provisions allowing the department to discipline officers who are guilty of conduct unbecoming an officer, a term frequently used by the uniformed services, but the term is difficult to define. It is vague and is used as a catch-all by police departments who can find no specific rule to apply to a situation, so it has been defined on a case-by-case basis.

A case involving an Ohio state trooper illustrates the problem. It was raining heavily on October 24, 1988 when the officer pulled a woman over for speeding. Later, she accused the officer of punching her in the face after he asked her to sit next to him in his patrol car.

The state disciplined the officer for "conduct unbecoming" an officer because the highway patrol code of ethics requires officers to be "courteous at all times." The regulations define "conduct unbecoming" as follows: "A member may be charged with conduct unbecoming an officer in the following situations: (1) For all disorders and neglects to the prejudice of good order and discipline. (2) For conduct that brings discredit to the Ohio State Highway Patrol and any of its members."

At the arbitration hearing, the grievant testified that when the woman would not roll down her window to talk to him, he ordered her to sit in his car. When he asked for her license, she touched his face with it. This startled him, so that his "arm came up in a defensive position and [his] hand brushed across her face." His intention had been to protect himself, not to hit her. He explained that he apologized to the woman. The grievant admitted that he did not report the incident to his supervisor, because he did not think it was important. He pointed to his prior good record. He had even received three letters from members of the public, praising his conduct.

The woman told a different story. She had been upset about having to move to the officer's car because it was raining, but when the officer asked for her license, she gave it to him. She said that she placed it on the arm rest between the seats, in a looping motion which she demonstrated to the arbitrator. She said that she had not touched the officer. The license was never less than seven to twelve inches from his face, but, she said, he had reacted violently, shoving his clenched fist into her face. She had been afraid, because she saw no reason for his action.

The State put the grievant's disciplinary record into evidence. It showed one written reprimand and three verbal reprimands, and the written reprimand was for conduct unbecoming an officer. None of the reprimands involved complaints from the public.

Arbitrator Patricia Thomas Bittel is a permanent arbitrator for the Ohio Highway Patrol and the Fraternal Order of Police. After listening to the evidence, she decided that the State had just cause to suspend the officer. The woman probably did touch the officer with her license, which may have caused a reaction by the officer, but while such a reaction might have been appropriate for an average person, the State had a right to expect more from a trained trooper. The officer's grievance was denied.

POLICE OFFICERS MUST TELL THE TRUTH

All police departments expect their officers to tell the truth, and if a police officer is caught in a lie, discipline is inevitable, and arbitrators usually support such penalties. Telling a lie is like stealing from the department, no matter how trivial a falsification it may seem. Police departments must be able to rely on their officers. Unless they can trust them, it would be impossible to uphold the law and to overcome the influences of organized crime.

The grievant in a case in Houston, Texas was a five year veteran. On April 27, 1988 he was assigned to the 7:00 PM to 3:00 AM shift. Arriving early for his shift, he checked out the keys for a squad car. Without waiting for the roll call, he drove to the police department's emergency communications division where he planned to deliver a cheesecake to his girlfriend on the switchboard, but he was intercepted by a sergeant, who ordered him out of the control room. The officer went upstairs to a break room where he was again confronted by the sergeant, and they exchanged some bitter words.

The sergeant filed a complaint. As a result, the officer was disciplined for being disrespectful to a superior officer. He also was charged with telling a lie, because he had told the sergeant that he had permission to be absent from roll call. When the sergeant called to verify that statement, he learned that the officer did not have permission to go downtown. The City also charged the officer with attempting to intimidate the sergeant by writing down his name on a note pad during their confrontation.

The department suspended the officer for five days. At a subsequent arbitration, the issue was whether or not the City had just cause to discipline the grievant and whether or not the penalty was appropriate.

The grievant attempted to explain away the incident. He said that he had received a subpoena from the district attorney's office that he needed to clarify, and on his way, he had decided to drop off the cheesecake. He did not lie to the sergeant and left soon after their conversation.

Arbitrator William L. McKee was convinced that the grievant had gone downtown without approval, but he also discovered that it was quite common for officers to miss roll call without prior approval and that no disciplinary action had ever been taken for such absences. The grievant had told his desk officer about his trip before leaving the station, and he had also called the dispatcher while en route.

The sergeant in the communications center was the only one who could testify about what the grievant had said, and the grievant disputed his testimony. The arbitrator found no reason to favor the sergeant's testimony. In his award, the arbitrator said, "Given the life threatening situations that police officers face on a regular basis, it is also difficult to fathom that the sergeant was intimidated when the officer wrote down his name on a note pad."

The arbitrator decided that the grievant was guilty but not of untruthfulness or intimidation, and he ordered those charges to be removed from the grievant's file. The grievant did miss roll call and did act disrespectfully. These were serious infractions, McKee said; therefore, he upheld the City's suspension of the grievant for five days.

A LACK OF INTEGRITY

A somewhat more serious case arose in Reno, Nevada where a sergeant with seventeen years on the force was accused of misrepresenting himself. The case began with a local fire on October 10, 1988. One of the officers, who was diverting traffic away from the scene, encountered a local television reporter named Pamela Drum. She argued with the officer about where she could park her sports car. The officer gave her a ticket for refusing to obey his directions and for not having her driver's license.

On the morning of Drum's trial, a City attorney was approached by a man in civilian clothes who explained that he was a policeman, which was not unusual. Prosecuting attorneys often speak with interested police officers before a case goes to trial. The officer told the attorney that he had just spoken to Ms. Drum, and he encouraged him to dismiss the case. The City attorney was under the impression that the officer was speaking for the police department. This was the sergeant later accused of misrepresentation.

The attorney dismissed the case, but later the complaining officer told him to proceed. The case went to trial, but subsequently the charges were dropped by a municipal court judge.

When the police department discovered what the sergeant had done, he was charged with violating a city ordinance. He was also terminated for "obstructing a public officer in the performance of his duty" by telling the City attorney that the police wanted the case dropped. According to the City, the sergeant had impaired his reputation as a police officer. The criminal conviction was later dismissed on appeal.

The union explained that the grievant was a friend of Ms. Drum, but he also knew the traffic officer involved. He had wanted to avoid a court room confrontation between them. He was only trying to avoid a misunderstanding.

Professor Paul D. Staudohar of California State University was the arbitrator. In his opinion the grievant's intentions were not reprehensible, but he should have made it clear that he was acting as a friend, not as a representative of the police department. The grievant was not a good witness. He initially testified that he was in court to look into a case of drunk driving, but the testimony of his lieutenant cast doubt on that story. Then the grievant acknowledged that he had not been truthful, and his record showed an earlier incident of untruthfulness.

When examined as a whole, the arbitrator concluded, the grievant's behavior was inappropriate. "Police officers are expected to have a higher level of integrity than the grievant demonstrated. Coupled with his 1985 suspension for dishonesty, the current episode becomes more serious. While he may have meant well, his actions were faulty. Thus, the City had just cause to discipline the grievant." However, the arbitrator said, the penalty was too extreme. The grievant's seventeen year record was fairly good, and his behavior was "not sufficiently egregious" to justify termination. Under the principles of progressive discipline, a forty-five day suspension was enough to punish him for overzealousness.

This was a three person panel, with one person, an investigator from the district attorney's office, appointed by the union, and another, a captain from the county sheriff's office, appointed by the City. The department's arbitrator filed a dissent, saying that the grievant should be demoted, as well as suspended. These party-appointed panels are increasingly rare in labor arbitration. A single arbitrator, mutually selected or appointed by a neutral agency, is far less cumbersome and expensive. Most of the cases in this book were heard and decided by a single arbitrator.

ANOTHER DETECTIVE MEDDLING IN A COURT CASE

Arbitrators are sometimes unable to get to the bottom of a case. In a case from Erie, Pennsylvania a City attorney was shot in his office on February 11, 1988. At the hospital, where they were trying to save him, the operating room supervisor handed the two police officers assigned to the case a bag containing the attorney's belongings, including two vials containing narcotics. When the two officers returned to the police station, a detective with twenty-five years' service spoke to them about the case. The detective's lieutenant called him aside and warned him that he was not assigned to the case.

Later, the detective again talked to one of the men while he was taking a statement from witnesses. The detective said that he knew a secretary in the attorney's office, and he would see if he could obtain the lawyer's file on one of the potential suspects to see if it contained any information about the shooting. The detective also volunteered to develop a photo lineup to show witnesses for identification, because he knew the suspect.

The detective advised the officers not to send the drugs out for chemical analysis, because no one knew whether the attorney would live or die. An argument on that subject broke out between one of the officers and the detective, and the officers filed a complaint about his interference.

After an investigation, the City decided that the detective had interfered with the investigation. In Pennsylvania, unbecoming conduct is any activity that adversely affects the efficiency of the department, and, according to the City, the detective's actions constituted such conduct.

Although he had no responsibility for the case, he had made other officers believe that he was involved. Police officers are expected to follow the chain of command, and the detective disregarded his supervisor's orders. This could not be taken lightly; therefore, he was suspended for five days. His union filed a grievance.

The grievant admitted that he had advised the two officers not to order the tests, because he thought there might be no need for a test. If the attorney died, there would be no prosecution for possession of drugs, and, in fact, the man had died.

Arbitrator Ronald F. Talarico is a full-time arbitrator. It was clear to him that the grievant wanted to be involved in the investigation, because the grievant knew that this case was "hot," and he had wanted to work on it. The arbitrator pointed out that in many police departments, officers who are not officially assigned to a case can volunteer their services, and this is what the grievant had tried to do. The question was whether or not he had interfered with the investigation.

When asked whether or not he was assigned to the case, the grievant had taken some licenses, and this had led the officers to believe that he was working on the case. One can quibble about the semantics of "being on the case," but Talarico was convinced that the grievant had tried to create a false impression that he was assigned to the case. As a twenty-four year veteran, he should have known better. He had overstepped the boundaries and impeded the department's operations. This was conduct unbecoming a police officer, and his grievance was denied.

At no point in the arbitrator's opinion were the grievant's motivations explained. Was he protecting the reputation of the city attorney? Was he attempting to inject himself into a high profile investigation? Or was he involved in some other way?

FALSIFYING POLICE RECORDS

Falsifying records is regarded as a serious infraction by most employers, and police departments are particularly strict in that connection. They expect accuracy.

An officer in Milwaukee was suspended for falsifying time cards. In 1989, he was working as a desk sergeant on the late shift in the Metropolitan Division. For fifteen years, he was on street patrol, and he had been a sergeant since 1987. Only recently had he been brought inside.

On July 23, he was scheduled to work from 7:00 PM to 3:00 AM. Two clerks usually worked with the sergeant at the desk, preparing time cards. On July 23, one took four hours compensatory time, leaving the other to work alone. The sergeant also left two hours early, noting that fact in his duty report, but his time card showed that he had worked the full eight hour shift, and he was paid for eight hours.

The City pointed out that the grievant was responsible for the accuracy of the time cards of seventy or more officers, and he was expected to review the cards and approve them as being accurate. The work rules stated that "no member of the Department shall make false official reports or knowingly enter or cause to be entered in any department books or records any inaccurate, false, or improper information."

The City gave the grievant a five day suspension for falsifying his time card. This was later reduced to a two day suspension; nevertheless, a grievance was filed.

The union claimed that the grievant had been unjustly disciplined. At the arbitration hearing, the union argued that the suspension should be removed from his record. The grievant's mistake was inadvertent, because he had instructed the clerk to note his absence on his time card, but she had neglected to do so. He had not attempted to steal two hours' pay. According to the union, the grievant took a three day vacation following the incident and afterwards was assigned to a different job. He simply forgot to record his compensation time from ten days earlier.

The department claimed that the grievant had violated a rule and some sort of discipline was justified. Arbitrator Milo G. Flaten, Jr., formerly with the Wisconsin Employment Relations Commission, had to decide whether or not the department had acted with just cause. Did the grievant falsify his time card?

The arbitrator said that the City's approach was "tantamount to liability regardless of fault." An inadvertent mistake had been made. The clerk forgot to change the grievant's time card, because the clerk was working alone and carrying on a radio conversation with officers on the street. The grievant had other things on his mind, because he was leaving work early because of family problems. The arbitrator was convinced that the grievant's failure was not intentional.

The grievant had been employed for many years without a blemish on his record and that long service weighed in his favor. On that basis, the arbitrator upheld the grievance, ordering that he be reimbursed for back pay and the suspension be removed from the record.

The City of Milwaukee was probably not happy with such a decision. The sergeant had been responsible for time sheets, and his time sheet resulted in his being overcompensated. Is it surprising that the sergeant was again assigned to patrol duty?

A CASE OF DISHONESTY

Dishonesty frequently results in termination or indefinite suspension, which means the same thing. The City of Denton in Texas indefinitely suspended a police officer for signing a false statement in the summer of 1988. The City had posted an opening for sergeant and announced there would be a civil service promotional examination on September 9, 1988 at the Texas Women's University in Denton. The notice described the qualifications and salary for the position, and it stated that applications to take the exam had to be filed by no later than noon on September 8, 1988.

One officer updated an earlier application and took the examination. His score was eighty-eight, the highest score, but that examination was subsequently declared invalid. A second examination was scheduled for Friday, December 16, 1988. Once again, the notice said that applications had to be on file no later than noon on December 15, 1988.

On December 15, 1988 someone from the police personnel department called the captain to inform him that the rules would be enforced and that anyone who had not signed up by noon would not be allowed to take the test. The captain posted a notice, but the officer never saw it because he was at home studying for the examination.

Another officer was working the front desk that evening. At about 6 PM, she received a telephone call from a friend in the personnel department who said that the personnel director in charge of the test wanted to know why the officer who had won the last competition had not signed up again for the sergeant's examination. The director told the officer that, "You have to follow the rules and the rules say that you got to sign up." Her friend agreed to do the paperwork, so that the officer would be on the list.

The desk officer said that she would call him, but a moment later, her friend called back and said, "You don't need to be spreading it around that we're doing this, OK?" The officer responded, "I never heard it," unaware that the tail end of her conversation was overheard by another police officer.

That evening, the desk officer called the grievant at home, telling him that she had talked to personnel. She said, "I got a way around it. It seems that I've got friends over there. All you have to do is call them and they'll fix it." The officer then called the personnel office, and his application was placed on file.

Thirteen police officers took the examination on December 16, 1988. The original winner and another officer tied for the highest grade with a score of eighty-six. Two other officers who had not signed up were allowed to take the examination.

The Civil Service Commission received a complaint from an officer who had not met the deadline and did not take the test. He complained that walk-ins were allowed to take the test, even though there was an official notice that they would not be permitted to do so. He complained that he had been denied an opportunity to take the test. As a result, the Civil Service Commission asked the City to certify which of the individuals on the eligibility list had submitted their applications at or before noon, December 15, 1988. The list would be resubmitted to the Civil Service Commission for people who met the application criteria.

On January 24, 1989 the original winner met with the police chief to discuss the situation. He affirmed that he had submitted his application before noon on December 15, 1988 and signed a certification.

There was a rumor in the department that someone had overheard the telephone conversations between the desk officer and the personnel office the evening before the examination, and an investigation took place to determine the validity of the rumor. The chief asked the original winner whether or not he understood the consequences of his certification, but the officer was adamant that he had signed the certification correctly.

The Denton police department keeps a master tape of all telephone calls to the police department over a twenty-four hour period. The communications supervisor searched the tapes for the evening of December 15, 1988 and found the conversations on the tape between the two officers and the personnel director.

At a subsequent hearing, the officer said that he thought that filing for the earlier test satisfied the requirement and that because there had been no changes in his application, he believed that he was eligible to take the test when he signed the certification. In almost six years of service, he had never done anything to warrant disciplinary action. He said that the personnel department had consistently bungled the administration of the tests and that he had not been notified of the deadline.

To arbitrator Edmund W. Schedler, Jr., an attorney who also teaches at Southern Methodist University, the issue was whether or not the City had just cause to suspend the officer for dishonesty. Schedler concluded that the officer misunderstood the situation and that the procedures for the test had been bungled. It was unfair for the City to enforce the deadline when some people who intended to take the test were unable to sign up. For example, the grievant was at home studying, which was not fair.

However, the City's failure did not totally justify the officer's actions. The officer had lied and damaged his reputation. The grievant should have made a disclosure of the telephone calls when asked to sign the certificate on January 24, 1989.

The arbitrator pointed out that the certification was not ambiguous. The grievant knew that he was too late to get on the list, but if he called personnel, they would put him on the list. He knew that he had subverted the purpose of the deadline for the examination, and he did not respond truthfully.

After carefully considering the evidence, the arbitrator found just cause to suspend the grievant and denied the grievance. The moral of the story is that lying is dangerous for police officers. Whatever else they do, they should tell the truth.

STEALING WHILE ON DUTY

Stealing is also taken seriously by police departments, even when the amounts are trivial. An identification technician working with the Miami police force was terminated for pilferage. On May 2, 1989 he had been sent to an Amoco Food Mart, the scene of an armed robbery and shooting, to gather evidence. The City claimed that while there he had consumed food and beverages belonging to the store, and a videotape showed the officer removing food from the shelves. According to the department, he did not pay or offer to pay for the food. A police officer at the scene testified that she saw the grievant consuming food that belonged to the store, and the City charged that the officer had lied about his actions. Because the grievant's job required him to testify in criminal cases, any lack of credibility destroyed his value as an employee.

At an arbitration hearing on July 31, 1990, the union pointed out that the City had the burden of proving beyond a reasonable doubt each element of the offense. Mere suspicions were not sufficient to support discharge for theft. The videotape, with the grievant's back to the camera and his hands out of sight, did not clearly establish guilt. The only person in the picture who took food from the shelves was someone other than the grievant and that person was neither interviewed nor disciplined. None of the other police officers present at the time of the incident were interviewed. The City's investigation was extremely sloppy.

The City also relied on the grievant's refusal to take a lie detector test, but the union pointed out that under Florida law no adverse presumption can be drawn from such a refusal.

Arbitrator Lloyd L. Byars ordered the grievant reinstated. The grievant had an excellent work record, and the videotape did not show the grievant consuming food and drink. Although he drank something, there was no evidence that it was from the store, and no one saw him take food. In fact, there was no testimony that food was missing from the store. The arbitrator agreed with the union that the grievant's refusal to take a polygraph test was not relevant, since such a refusal is not an admission of guilt. Based on the lack of evidence, the grievant was reinstated.

NEGLIGENCE IN THE LINE OF DUTY

Police officers are held to high standards, and when dealing with slippery criminals, they must always be on the alert. A female officer in Chicago responded to a call from a food market on July 9, 1988 where a shoplifter had been apprehended. The officer and her partner apprehended the man, who had taken a package of meat without paying for it. He was placed in handcuffs.

After walking their prisoner to the car, the grievant took off the cuffs, placed the prisoner in the back of the car, and sat in the front seat. She thought the car doors were locked. The prisoner slouched down, and she told him to sit up, but he said he was sick. Suddenly, the prisoner opened the door and escaped, and the grievant was unable to catch him.

Several weeks later, she found the prisoner and arrested him, but afterwards, the department decided that she had been negligent and suspended her for a day. Her union filed a grievance.

George Roumell, the arbitrator, heard the case. He is one of the busiest arbitrators in Michigan. After listening to the testimony, he concluded that the grievant had been negligent. He felt that an armed police officer should be able to maintain custody and that she had no good explanation for her failure. Roumell denied the grievance. The City had properly suspended the officer for one day.

FAILURE TO COOPERATE WITH THE
MEDICAL EXAMINER

Another female officer was disciplined for failing to cooperate with the city medical examiner in a suicide investigation. Police officers are supposed to be able to deal with other city agencies, and when they get into arguments, they may be criticized for being uncooperative. In a case in Galveston, Texas that is what happened.

The officer was sent to the scene of a juvenile's suicide attempt on July 16, 1988, but when she arrived she found the boy being loaded into an ambulance, so she went to the hospital to collect information for her report. She was expected to report on the condition of the victim and the weapon used, and to interview any witnesses.

The boy died on the way to the hospital. In the emergency room, the officer located his body, which was being attended by medical staff. She needed further information from the ambulance technicians to complete her report, but she was told that they had left. As she rushed out to catch them, she was intercepted by a woman who asked her about the suicide. She brushed off the questions, but later, she learned that the woman was the City's medical examiner.

The officer found the ambulance technicians, collected the necessary information, and returned to the emergency room to obtain additional information from the attending physician. With that data, she went back to the police station to complete her paperwork, where she was told by her sergeant that the medical examiner had complained about her behavior, claiming that she had been rude and had refused to provide information about the case. She returned to the hospital at once and provided full information to the medical examiner.

The City suspended the officer for three days, contending that her behavior had hindered the investigation of the medical examiner. The rule was that officers were to remain with a body until the medical examiner contacted them, at least according to one police department witness.

There had been earlier complaints about the grievant's being rude. For example, a pastor claimed that while investigating a complaint about loud music, the grievant had barged into his church during a service. Another person had complained that she had been indifferent to a neighborhood problem involving juveniles. Also, the grievant had sometimes failed to notify the authorities in advance when she was unable to be in court. For some of these earlier complaints, a memo had been placed in her file.

At the arbitration, the grievant claimed that the incident in the hospital had been blown out of proportion. When she returned to the hospital, the first thing she did was apologize to the medical examiner for not recognizing her. She had not noticed her in the crowded room. Also, she had to catch the emergency technicians before they left, because she needed their information for her report. Afterwards, she returned to the emergency room to speak to the attending physician. If the medical examiner had been there, she would have given her the information.

Arbitrator William L. McKee was selected from an American Arbitration Association (AAA) list in accordance with Texas law. He showed some sympathy for the grievant's explanation but had to decide whether or not her three day suspension was for just cause.

He saw a similarity between the two women. Both had to obtain information to complete their assignments: The medical examiner needed the police report for her file, and the grievant had to obtain the facts for her report. They both encountered difficulties in collecting information, and both women took their jobs seriously. They were intense people, perhaps too intense, and they were likely to clash when their job responsibilities conflicted.

The arbitrator was not convinced that police officers were instructed to remain with the body of a suicide until they reported to a medical examiner. All things considered, the evidence did not persuade him that the grievant' had been unreasonably abrupt. He reduced the grievant's three days' suspension to one day. The discipline had been too harsh, considering the circumstances.

Was this award based on compromise, a result that labor arbitrators are sometimes accused of? Why didn't McKee dismiss the entire grievance? This is a perennial issue among labor arbitrators. Must they abide by the penalty imposed by the employer or can they reduce a suspension as McKee did in this case?

WHEN TO TAKE A DRUNK TO A HOSPITAL

In Philadelphia, the police are supposed to take a drunk to a hospital if the person is "semi-conscious or unconscious." On the face of it, the rule seems clear. In practice, the clarity evaporates, as it did in the following case.

On January 16, 1989 two officers were operating a patrol wagon when the radio dispatcher told them to pick up someone who was intoxicated. They found the man handcuffed, sitting on the ground and having difficulty holding up his head. The arresting officer told them to take the man to the twenty-second district station house. Although the man was staggering, he could walk under his own power. In the police station, he was booked, put in a cell, and charged with intoxication. As the two officers were about to leave, the station's turn-key told them that the man had passed out, and they were told to take the man to a local hospital, where he eventually died.

The two officers were given five days' suspension for failing to take the prisoner directly to the hospital. The Fraternal Order of Police filed a grievance.

Arbitrator Andrew S. Price heard the case. Two questions were involved: Had the officers violated the departmental rule? And if so, did the department have just cause to suspend them? The case turned on the meaning of "semi-conscious." When the man was picked up, was he conscious or semi-conscious?

Price assumed that the police department's directive did not require officers to take every drunk to a hospital, which had never been the case in Philadelphia. Police officers often delivered drunks to their station house and had never been criticized for doing so. The language of the directive had been interpreted liberally. Price concluded that semi-conscious must have been intended to mean something more than being drunk, but the City's witnesses were unable to define the term.

Price decided that the grievant's actions were reasonable. Because the prisoner did not lose consciousness until he was placed in a cell, the arbitrator decided that the department had no reason to discipline the grievants. The City was told to remove all references to the suspension and to pay the grievants for the five days they had been penalized.

Police officers are not physicians, but they often encounter people who are under the influence of a drug or alcohol or who may be suffering from illnesses that have similar symptoms. Whether to take such people to a hospital, to a station house, or to leave them with friends is a decision that police make constantly. If they guess wrong, they may be in trouble. A practical solution is to allow them discretion. Who is better able to make such decisions than an experienced police officer who is familiar with life in the streets?

THE UNOBSERVED RULE

As was emphasized earlier, police departments are prolific rule makers, but many of the provisions are ambiguous and hard to apply. Such rules may be difficult to define, particularly if a rule has never been enforced or has been intermittently enforced; or, if an officer was never informed of the rule, it is unfair to require such compliance. Many police grievances involve the latter situation: An officer is penalized for breaking a rule that he or she never knew existed.

On December 21, 1987, two policemen from the small town of Belleville, Michigan were on patrol in their squad car at 3:00 o'clock in the morning. Belleville contains two square miles, and it is bisected by a major expressway, I-94, but the expressway entrance and exit are just outside Belleville limits. The police share a radio dispatch system with another small township.

A message came across the radio that morning, asking police to be on the alert for two automobiles that were involved in a shooting at a White Castle restaurant in a township outside of Ann Arbor. The vehicles were a red Pathfinder and a white Nissan, and both were said to be escaping eastbound on I-94.

In response, the officers drove to the Belleville exit to a location designated by the state police as the best lookout point for observing traffic on I-94. The two officers waited there for about fifteen minutes. When no contact was made, they drove eastbound on I-94 to return to Belleville. They came up on a Van Buren Township squad car occupied by two officers, and they parked next to each other to discuss their strategy.

As the Belleville officers drove away, one of them said, "If you need us, give us a holler." Then, they drove back towards Belleville.

While still outside the town limits, the Belleville officers heard a radio message from the Van Buren cruiser, saying that it was following a red Pathfinder. The message concluded with, "Do you copy 871," the number of the Belleville vehicle.

The Belleville officers assumed that the Van Buren officers were asking for their assistance. They sped to I-94, heading east. Soon, they heard the Van Buren officer ask, "871, could you bring up the rear?" But during the pursuit, the Van Buren officer repeatedly asked the Belleville officers to "back off." The officers from Belleville were somewhat confused. The Pathfinder was apprehended about six miles east on I-94 beyond Belleville.

On the following day, the Van Buren chief of police wrote the following letter:

I am writing to you about an incident that occurred on December 21, 1987 in the early morning hours because I would certainly want such a situation brought to my attention. How you choose to address this information is none of my business and I would never follow up.

This incident arose out of a shooting in Pittsfield Township. A Van Buren officer located the vehicle on Eastbound I-94. He was coordinating apprehension with Romulus P.D. and Wayne County Sheriff's Department when your officers arrived on the scene. You should be advised that they were not requested nor was their assistance needed. This occurred on I-94 near Merriman, miles from your jurisdiction.

By all accounts, once on the scene, your officers violated standard procedure for felony traffic stop, ignoring basic vehicle and officer placement, thereby endangering not only themselves but other officers.

In view of the fact that this is not the first problem of this nature we've brought to your attention I feel I have no alternative other than to request the following: unless they are specifically called upon for back-up I request your officers refrain from responding to scenes in the Township.

Do not interpret this to mean that we would hesitate to respond to your community if we are requested. We wouldn't. We will, however, be very careful to render only that specific service needed and not interfere with the execution of your standard operating procedures. We request the same in return from your personnel.

After investigating the incident, the Belleville police department disciplined the two officers by suspending them for three days without pay. A grievance was filed, and arbitrator George T. Roumell, Jr. had to decide whether or not the officers should have been punished.

The violated rule was not to leave city limits without permission. Admittedly, there was no direct authority for the officers going to the lookout point at I-94 and to Belleville Road, however, the radio message did indicate that this was not an ordinary situation. A shooting was mentioned, suggesting that the persons involved in the vehicle could be dangerous. These experienced officers believed that immediate action was necessary.

Although the officers were technically in violation, testimony showed that Belleville officers had sometimes been asked to catch vehicles traveling on I-94.

Roumell decided that the two officers were not guilty of misconduct. Before employees can be punished for breaking a rule, they must be told what is expected of them. This is not to say that the department must issue regulations covering every possible situation, which would be unrealistic, but in a situation like this, the department's policy should be made known before disciplinary action is invoked.

FAILURE TO FILE A REPORT

It is frustrating for a police officer to be disciplined for violating a rule that has not been previously enforced or one that is too ambiguous to be properly understood. For example, a nineteen year veteran of the Brook Park Police Department was given a three day suspension for failing to file a report on an incident "requiring official police attention."

On September 1, 1987 the officer had almost finished his 7 AM to 3 PM shift and was in the motor pool servicing his patrol car for the next shift. While there, he received a radio call from the police dispatcher. The officer's daughter had telephoned from a K-Mart store in Middleburg Heights, a nearby town where she was working. She had been harassed by someone who had assaulted her once before, and she asked her father to come to her rescue.

The officer asked for permission to drive his patrol car to Middleburg Heights, and the sergeant, aware of the situation, granted his request. On his way, the officer was told by the radio dispatcher that the man who had bothered his daughter was now in an automobile parked in front of a nearby fast food restaurant. The officer radioed the Middleburg Heights police, asking them to send a car to the scene. When the officer arrived at the scene, he saw the automobile his daughter had described, but when he asked the driver for identification, a passenger in the car began accusing him of harassment.

The officer's daughter and a police officer from Middleburg Heights arrived soon afterwards. The daughter identified the passenger as the man who had assaulted her, and she said that she would press charges.

The Middleburg Heights officer told the man that he was under arrest, and a struggle broke out. To assist the arresting officer, the Brook Park officer held the prisoner's arm and forced him onto the hood of the patrol car while he was being handcuffed.

The Brook Park officer did not report the incident in his police radio log or in his duty report, nor was any report made to the Middleburg Heights department, nor did either department ask for a report.

Almost a year later, on August 12, 1988, the Brook Park chief of police came across a newspaper article describing a law suit filed by the person arrested for assault, battery, and wrongful arrest against both cities, the Brook Park officer, his daughter, and the Middleburg Heights officer. The mayor of Brook Park, when notified of the article, asked the police chief about the incident. The chief could find nothing in his files, and he had never been told of the incident. The chief asked the Brook Park officer to file a written report, which was submitted on August 22, 1988. On October

26, the chief sent him a disciplinary letter and suspended him for three days for failing to submit a report at the time of the incident.

The officer's union filed an arbitration, pointing out that the rule was too ambiguous to be enforced. It was impossible to tell when a report was required and, based on past practice, the officer had not thought that a report was necessary.

The City took the position that its rule was reasonable. The grievant should have known that what started out as a personal matter became something that required official police attention when he helped to arrest someone in another jurisdiction. After nineteen years, the officer should have known that such an incident would require an official report.

Arbitrator Norman Prusa was asked to decide whether or not the rule could be enforced. He read the rule with great care, and its obscurity was obvious. The testimony of the grievant's superiors was equally ambiguous. One said that reports were made only when Brook Park police provided assistance to police in other jurisdictions and only when a report was requested. The other stated that he had never been required to file such a report when he worked with other police departments. The arbitrator upheld the grievance, ordering that the grievant be paid for the three lost days.

SUMMARY

It is appropriate for police officers to be disciplined for violating departmental rules but not when the rules are unclear or enforced in a capricious way. As the cases in this chapter illustrate, police officers deserve to be told in advance what rules and regulations must be observed and should be treated with justice and equality.

Among the many rules that are imposed upon American police officers, at least some are totally unfair. Arbitrators are well placed to sift the wheat from the chaff, because they are familiar with other areas of employment. Ambiguous rules that are capriciously imposed upon police officers add still another level of stress to an already difficult job.

CHAPTER 9

The Purpose of Police Departments

For many Americans fear of violence is a major concern. Not everyone, of course, is worried because some people live in relatively secure suburbs or in small towns that are seemingly untouched by crime. But concerns about personal safety are poisoning large parts of the United States and creating an epidemic of fear. People in some neighborhoods are afraid to walk the streets at night, and children are kept home, because parents worry about their safety.

Business firms fret about the safety of their workers after dark. More private security guards are employed in the United States than police officers, and many cops work as private guards during their off-duty hours. The sale of electronic alarms, defensive firearms, and guard dogs also testifies to the growth of the security business—a market based on fear.

Every year, records are set for arrests and convictions, and more people are sentenced to prison in the United States than anywhere else in the world. The United States has the largest prison population in the world—over a million people. Why is this happening? Is it the fault of the police? Or does the entire criminal justice system need to be changed?

When communities were smaller and more intimate police officers walking their beat knew people in the neighborhood and could anticipate problems. Police were part of the community, where they maintained order and often were respected by the people they served. When an incident occurred, the officer might already know the people involved and could react to the situation, even if he was not on the scene when it happened. But American society has changed and it has become more complicated. Because of the size and complexity of many urban communities, much of the day-to-day contact between police and citizen has been lost.

THE RADIO DISPATCH SYSTEM OF POLICE RESPONSE

Most police departments currently rely on a rapid response system where calls come into a central telephone exchange and messages are sent by radio to patrol cars scattered throughout the city. Based on whatever information the telephone operator can glean from a caller, cars are assigned to an incident. The officers arrive at the scene ill-prepared for what they may face. They must size up the people involved and make raw assumptions about the facts. Snap judgments are the name of the game.

Responding officers are under pressure to act quickly. They are expected to get back on patrol as soon as possible and be ready for another assignment. Respond quickly, size up the situation, fix the immediate problem, then exit the scene: This is typical of modern police work. The theory behind this is that rapid response increases the chance of arrest, serves as a deterrent, and provides a satisfactory public service, but research shows otherwise.

Nevertheless, the rapid response is used by most urban police departments in the United States, even though critics say that there are better ways to provide police services and that reform is necessary. They point out that only a small percentage of reported crimes result in an arrest, and typically the police arrive after the perpetrator has left the scene. Also, there is a high level of public dissatisfaction with the present service.

THE CAUSES OF CRIME IN AN URBAN SOCIETY

The causes of violence in a society are complex, but surely the alienation and incompetence of so many young men in America's urban areas is one driving force. They cannot cope. Unable to hold a job, they steal or deal in drugs; unable to express themselves, they resort to violence; unhappy and unwell, they resort to alcohol or drugs.

Society responds by using the criminal law to enforce standards of social behavior, and the first instrument of the law is often a police officer responding to a complaint. The police arrest large numbers of people, turning them over to the criminal courts to be processed by the slow, grinding machinery of the law.

In New York City, thousands of young men are held in jail at Rikers Island under scandalous conditions, and similar, overcrowded facilities exist in many other cities. People who study the situation suspect that violence will continue to erupt so long as no serious effort is made to address the social problems.

Many of the young men convicted of crimes of violence are uneducated, functionally handicapped people who participate in illicit activities. Illegal drug sales and similar activities create a criminal atmosphere in their communities, and they have become a major target of police activity.

TARGET NUMBER ONE: DRUG SALES

If the government wants drug dealers to be arrested, that task becomes a priority for the local police. More people are arrested, and the workload of the criminal courts increase. With inadequate budgets, the courts respond by making greater use of plea bargaining and by committing more of their resources to handling drug cases.

In some municipalities, this is exactly what has happened. Police departments allocate more and more resources to enforcing the drug laws, and large numbers of young drug dealers are taken to court, where they receive harsh sentences and go to prison. At the end of the conveyor belt are overcrowded correctional facilities where all the prison cells are filled. The young men graduate from their incarceration hardened criminals and go back into the community to practice their trade.

This chapter concentrates on the front end of that conveyor belt by raising questions about police priorities. Is it sensible for the police to allocate so much of their attention to drug sales? Would it be better to stress more community-oriented functions, such as patrolling the streets, protecting the citizens, helping to resolve day-to-day controversies, and becoming part of municipal services?

Rather than arresting low level drug dealers, the police would cope with social emergencies and be responsive to the concerns of the public. In that role, the police officer would be trained to resolve disputes that might otherwise result in conflict. Police officers would use the resources of other public agencies to help people to cope with potential problems.

THE POLICE AS A SOCIAL AGENCY

Police departments would be converted into service organizations under this system, whereby they would be helping to improve the quality of community life, encouraging citizen involvement, working with neighborhood groups, and coordinating with public agencies. Crime would be viewed as a community problem.

If crime is a social aberration, its cure can be found within the community. The primary effort should be to provide opportunities for young people and give them a chance for a meaningful life. Many young people cannot express themselves. They are incapable of engaging in the rough and tumble of modern life. They do not know how to carry out normal transactions or how to verbalize their disagreements with people so they turn to violence. By helping them to express themselves before they are committed to a life of crime, we can strengthen their ability to deal with problems and help them to operate in the larger community.

THE CORROSIVE EFFECT OF THE CURRENT DRUG POLICY

The emphasis on convictions and incarceration is having a caustic effect on the constitutional rights of people apprehended by the police. Search and seizures are increasingly common, as are drug busts, and more arrests are being made. Because much of this activity takes place in poor neighborhoods, it only comes to the attention of middle-class Americans on the evening news.

Criminal courts handle millions of cases where police officers identify and testify against people they have arrested, many of whom are adolescents and minorities accused of selling drugs or stealing to obtain money to buy drugs. Overwhelmed by the mass of cases, urban courts cannot provide trials to more than a small percentage of these. So most people who are charged with such crimes admit to a lesser charge to avoid being held in custody awaiting trial. This kind of plea bargaining frustrates the police officer who must appear in court but seldom sees the violator tried or convicted. In some cases, innocent suspects confess rather than wait for trial, and hardened criminals are offered a lesser sentence than they deserve.

Police officers know how this so-called "justice system" works, and they find their role demeaning. Officers soon recognize the inequities, the inappropriate court procedures, and the influence of lawyers retained by organized crime. Cops become cynical, because justice seems corrupt, if not blind. A zealous cop is humiliated and may wonder who is on trial. A police officer becomes frustrated, waiting around for the apprehended person to be brought into court, identified, and processed, knowing that nine out of ten will never be tried but rather will accept some lesser plea offered by the prosecutor. How hard it must be for the police officer to see such a person go free!

The drug industry offers plenty of entry-level positions, and because many dealers become addicted or are picked up by the police, there are constant openings. These unemployed young men, often addicted to drugs and needing money to pay for their habit, have created a dangerous environment in many neighborhoods, particularly when combined with deadly weapons that are freely available in the United States.

These problems exist, but we only become aroused when we suffer personally. Little has been done about the underlying social problems, and the national leadership has focused its attention on the illegal drug industry. The local police have been encouraged to go after local drug dealers. Drug raids, the prosecution of street sellers, the use of armed enforcement units, and undercover agents—these are the grist of the nightly news. They enhance the macho, aggressive activities of police departments and encourage further violence with the support of the federal government. The war against drugs may have become more of a threat than the drugs themselves.

THE INTERNAL WAR

The United States is at war with itself. The police are fighting a well-organized, politically protected, criminal drug industry, and the cops are not winning. In many neighborhoods, drug dealers have taken over. Drugs have become the driving force behind pilferage, hold-ups, auto theft, and burglaries. Cops see that they are caught in the middle: accused of violence by drug dealers and their customers, investigated by their own department, and criticized by the press.

In Japan, the homicide rate is less than 1 per 100,000. In New York City, the 1989 rate was 22.7 per 100,000. There were over 20,000 homicides in the United States in 1990, and it is the leading cause of death for black males. Gunfire is increasingly common in many inner city neighborhoods. Television programs bring this story into American living rooms every evening.

Crime is not solely a police problem but rather a symptom of major problems in our society. If the United States were willing to provide adequate family planning, health services, education, and employment, future generations might avoid an increased growth of violent crime.

WHO ARE THE VICTIMS?

In general, the victims of violent crime come from the same neighborhoods as their assailants. They are mostly poor and often come from minority groups. According to the National Center for Health Statistics, in 1987 the homicide victim rate for blacks was 65.9 per 100,000; for whites, it was 10.9 per 100,000. Black males are frequent homicide victims. Statistics on other violent crimes, such as burglary and theft, also show the heavy burden on residents of high crime areas, which tend to be neighborhoods troubled with poverty, unemployment, and inadequate public services.

Certain minorities are involved in more than their share of crime. Young males commit most violent crimes, usually in the neighborhoods where they live. Accordingly, a substantial proportion of the inmates in prison are black, mostly young, males.

The prison population in the United States has steadily increased, from about 200,000 in 1970 to over 700,000 in 1990, and this does not include the people in jail awaiting trial. Police intervention in the drug distribution system is largely responsible, because this emphasis has increased both arrests and convictions.

Drug related crimes have dramatically increased, from a rate of 10.8 per 100,000 for sale or manufacture of heroin and cocaine in 1980, to 74.8 per 100,000 in 1988; and from 22.2 per 100,000 for possession, to 258.7 per 100,000 in 1988. The arrest of males for selling heroin or cocaine is six times higher than for females, for possession it is five times higher.

Crack, cocaine, and heroin are supplied by an illegal drug industry with vast manufacturing and distribution resources. The use of police power to crush that industry by enforcing harsh criminal laws has created a violent confrontation. Many low level drug dealers are also users, and these young men constitute the public enemies that police officers confront when attempting to stamp out drug sales. This concentration on the supply side of drug enforcement, with local police and federal agents attempting to identify, arrest, and imprison drug dealers, has distorted the police mission by emphasizing such activities as drug busts, undercover agents, and armed confrontations.

WHY ARE CURRENT POLICIES FAILING?

So far, there is no indication that the present policy has been effective. Some drugs have gone out of fashion, while crack and others seem more popular. The secondary effects of the emphasis on enforcement are clear: Multitudes of low level drug dealers, mostly young minority males, are being arrested and incarcerated.

It is difficult to be optimistic about putting such people in prison. Usually, they are released after a few months, more embittered than before, less employable because of their record, and potential recruits for organizations that need experienced staff for their illegal activities. The stiff sentences being imposed by criminal courts may be creating more vicious criminals for the future, rather than convincing individual drug dealers that they should take up another line of work.

Prisons are intended to keep dangerous individuals out of society. Incorrigible and violent people must be contained and protected from each other and from themselves. Maximum security prisons are required for dangerous inmates, but some people are sent to prison who do not pose a threat to society. Tax evaders, shoplifters, petty thieves, nonviolent drug addicts who sell small amounts of drugs in order to continue their use may not need to be incarcerated.

Unfortunately, our current policy is to put drug dealers in prison; therefore, the courts send thousands of young men to prison, placing them among hardened convicts. As a result, tax supported prisons produce brutal and dangerous criminals. Many inmates graduate back into the world of crime, because prisons breed alienation and social failure.

Two centuries ago, prisons were regarded as a social experiment. The idea was that solitary confinement, silence, drudgery, penitence, and chastity would redeem the criminal. Over the years, prisons have distanced themselves from the outside community, and billions of dollars are poured into them. People who are incarcerated emerge handicapped and embittered.

We admit defeat when we send someone to prison. To protect against the poison of prison life, we should divert many prisoners into community programs, work-release, probation, compensation of victims through restitution, and other forms of rehabilitation and punishment. For most offenders, correction should take place outside of prisons. Prisons should not be asked to do what they are incapable of doing.

THE ROLE OF CITIZEN COMPLAINTS

Some questions regarding the use of police remain, such as: Will there always be more citizen complaints? When people in high crime areas increasingly see police officers beating up drug dealers, how will they react? Will police supervision continue to defend officers against citizen complaints? Will the drug war continue to escalate?

The Rodney King incident in Los Angeles provided a highly publicized example of a confrontation between police officers and a young minority male who was badly beaten. Similar incidents are sometimes reported in urban newspapers or described on the evening news, but not always. Rodney King would have been unknown if a hand-held video camera had not been used to record his beating by four white police officers in the presence of twenty other officers.

Fairly common complaints that are filed include that a police officer has used more force than was necessary, that someone was beaten while being arrested, that unnecessary warning shots were fired by an officer, and that an innocent person was put up against a wall. These involve allegations that an officer has abused his power.

THE CRIMINAL JUSTICE SYSTEM AND THE POLICE

David Rudovsky points out that the public's fear of crime has given the police a license to "control the streets," which creates a "toleration of police abuse" and encourages the courts to legitimize police misbehavior, but there is not enough official data on police brutality to prove such allegations. Local departments do not send statistics to the FBI, so no one knows how common such incidents have become. According to a July, 1991 article in the *American Bar Association Journal* of some 2,028 excessive force complaints filed in San Francisco in 1985, only 22 were sustained. In 1990, 1,074 were filed, with 89 sustained. According to this article, in Los Angeles in 1985, 228 complaints were filed with only 8 sustained, while in 1990, 172 complaints were filed with 8 sustained. Only a few other high crime cities maintain statistics, and they report similar variations: Chicago (2,476 citizen complaints against police officers in 1990), Atlanta (800), Washington (415), Boston (180), and Miami (111). Because there are no objective standards for such statistics, they do not reveal much except that many Americans are complaining about the police.

To compare various cities it would be necessary to know how difficult it is for a citizen to file such a complaint. Must the citizen file in person or can he complain in writing or over the phone? What process is used by the police department to investigate and confirm the incident? The short answer is that nobody knows exactly how much excessive force is being used or where it is most common.

TOO MANY GUNS AVAILABLE

One justification for using force is to protect someone's life, and at least some of the people that police officers confront are armed. Can anyone criticize a cop for being trigger happy when handguns are so readily available?

John J. Curtin, former president of the American Bar Association (ABA), wrote in the July, 1991 *ABA Journal* that "the availability of guns is out of control." He cited a Department of Justice report that said that in 1990, 639,000 Americans had been confronted by criminals carrying handguns and that over 24,000 of them were killed or wounded.

The ABA supported a federal waiting period for purchasing guns and limiting the availability of military assault weapons. It seems hard to argue against these initiatives, and action is needed to remove the guns already in circulation. According to Curtin, there are about two million made-in-America assault guns, and millions of handguns circulating in the black market. Anybody can purchase a gun for cash.

Police organizations generally favor waiting periods and assault weapon prohibitions. Strong gun control legislation is overdue, because the present systems put too much pressure on the police.

People in other countries are shocked at the high rate of homicide in this country, and they wonder at the fact that Americans cannot walk their city streets at night in safety when undeveloped countries around the world are generally safe.

Residential segregation is part of the problem because the makeup of most urban police departments is dramatically different than the profile of many high crime neighborhoods. Although affirmative action programs have begun to change the numbers, the police still include a dominant percentage of white male officers.

Drug dealers are predominantly young minority males, many of whom are addicts, and they prey on their own kind and often on themselves. They are well armed and alienated from the society that the police are paid to protect, but they are part of the neighborhood, the sons and brothers of the people. The war against drugs is a war against these young men, and essentially it is a class or ethnic war.

CONCLUSION

This chapter has discussed some of the options available in the use of the police: Some options result from the chronic violence in high crime areas and others relate specifically to our national policy to stamp out drug sales. It has been suggested that a choice needs to be made between concentrating on law enforcement and emphasizing community service and that our current policies need to be revised. The dramatic increase in the prison population will only add to future law enforcement problems as inmates graduate back into the criminal life.

CHAPTER 10

Collective Bargaining and Interest Arbitration

Collective bargaining contracts define the terms of employment for members of the bargaining unit represented by a union, and when those employees are police officers, contract provisions reflect the unique nature of their work. Police work different hours than most other employees, often being assigned to particular shifts because policing is a twenty-four hour a day service. The conditions under which police officers work and the benefits that they receive are also different from those of many workers.

As public employees, police have somewhat more job security than most private employees. In some states, that security is provided by the state civil service law, which offers a secure status beyond that enjoyed by many workers, and when the officer is a member of a union, the just cause provision in the contract provides additional protection.

The arrangement between a police union and its department is contained in a negotiated contract, which is subject to the various applicable conditions in the state law. When a disagreement arises between a police union and a police department as to contract provisions, it can be resolved through the contract's grievance procedures or it can be renegotiated, but all resolutions are subject to state law.

The right to strike is almost always prohibited. The parties have the right to negotiate contract provisions, but if they cannot agree, they are usually required to arbitrate. Police unions, like other organizations, want better working conditions, as well as increased salaries. Therefore, union officials who bargain for police unions make much the same demands as other union officials: They want more money, plus better working conditions. In contrast, local voters would prefer to keep a lid on costs to hold down taxes, and like most employers, the police department is concerned about maintaining management control. These are interests that are commonly encountered on the collective bargaining table.

Individual salaries in police contracts usually depend on seniority and rank, a method favored by police unions. Parity with other uniformed services is a frequent source of controversy, because police officers believe that their job is more demanding and more dangerous than that of other municipal employees.

Police are an essential service, because without a vigilant police force, society would soon unravel, and people would lose confidence in the reliability of their environment. Once a neighborhood dissolves, dangerous influences infect the community, and in our polyglot American society, it does not take much to sweep away social inhibitions. Without police, the positive relationships of society would soon dissolve. In some parts of America, high crime neighborhoods are experiencing such chaotic conditions that there is little personal security.

Police forces in most American cities have become unionized. As a result—and because legislators fear strikes by the police more than any other form of work stoppage—many states have regulated police bargaining, often by providing some system of arbitration, in exchange for taking away the union's right to strike. These forms of arbitration are called interest arbitration.

In the 1970s this subject attracted widespread academic and editorial interest. Alarmists wrote that this use of arbitration would increase the salaries of police to such an extent that municipal budgets would be devastated. That has not happened, but it also cannot be demonstrated that interest arbitration has accomplished fair police wage settlements.

A comprehensive study by Professors Peter Feuille of the University of Illinois, John T. Delaney of Columbia, and Wallace Hendricks of the University of Illinois (in *Industrial Relations*, Vol. 24, No. 2 [Spring 1985]) that was based on 1,631 police union contracts concluded that the availability of interest arbitration was positively associated with favorable contracts for police unions. According to the study, the use of arbitration in any one year did not necessarily produce better results than were produced by negotiations. For example, from 1976 to 1981, police contracts became more favorable to the police in nonarbitration jurisdictions than where arbitration was available. The study did indicate that during the same period police contracts were becoming more uniform, which was viewed as favorable to police unions.

Factors other than the availability of interest arbitration may explain why police unions have been able to improve their compensation and working conditions in large communities. A union can be helpful to its members where the police face a hostile political environment, unusual fiscal restraint, an unreceptive electorate, or negative publicity, because then the right to arbitrate provides a useful alternative. Unless a union can engage in job action or make use of political influence, collective bargaining without the right to arbitrate may be an exercise in frustration.

Interest arbitration injects a new element, an impartial determination of a fair settlement. Some statutes give the arbitrator, or panel of arbitrators, the unlimited power to decide all bargaining issues while others limit the arbitrator to selecting between the parties' final bargaining demands. In any case, arbitrators are authorized to make an independent, but binding, determination. The result will reflect the arbitrator's expectation of where the parties would have reached an agreement if they had been allowed to do so, and will be a settlement that reflects their respective bargaining powers.

When preparing for negotiations in an interest arbitration, both parties review the results of earlier arbitrations and base their presentations on such comparisons. The availability of interest arbitration may influence their settlements, even when they never arbitrate. The costs of arbitration are also a factor. Neither the union nor the municipality want to invest in arbitration, if that is not necessary.

The researchers listed various factors that influence the bargaining strengths of police unions. The size of the city is generally related to higher salaries, and the demand for police services is also relevant, measured partially by the crime rate. High per capita income and high property value may also reflect a willingness to pay higher police salaries. These factors are related to the need for police protection and to the city's ability to pay. Police salaries are usually higher in urban areas than in rural communities, which is also the case for other municipal categories.

Other related factors are the history of the local bargaining relationship and the state bargaining law's definition of what can be negotiated. For example, if a city is authorized to engage in full-scale collective bargaining, it may be in a weaker position than if it can only "meet and confer." Some states authorize negotiations over wages, hours, and other terms and conditions of employment, while others exclude subjects such as those covered by the civil service law, pensions, or management rights.

To summarize, the Illinois research indicated that the highest police wage settlements were found in cities that are large, relatively wealthy, and with high crime rates.

The arbitration cases in this chapter describe situations where the dispute is between the union and the police department, rather than about an individual police officer. They provide examples of uneasy bargaining relationships where the exclusive role of the union has not been confirmed.

UNIONS FIGHTING FOR THE RIGHT TO ORGANIZE

Sometimes grievance arbitrations result from the competition between labor organizations. In states where the law does not provide exclusive bargaining rights to the labor organization that represents a majority of the employees this is always a possibility, and one that tends to weaken the unions involved.

In Corpus Christi, Texas the Police Officer's Association (POA) had an exclusive agreement with the City. On January 24, 1988 several officers asked for permission, on behalf of the POA, to install a bulletin board in police headquarters. Two days later, the chief of police also approved bulletin board space for the Fraternal Order of Police, a competing organization. In February, the chief reversed himself, denying the bulletin board to the Fraternal Order of Police in response to a grievance filed by the Police Officer's Association.

In March, the Fraternal Order also filed a grievance, protesting the chief's decision, combined with grievances filed by twenty-eight officers as individuals protesting the removal of the bulletin board. The twenty-eight grievances were consolidated into one proceeding for reasons of efficiency, but the Fraternal Order's grievance was not accepted because that organization had no contractual relationship with the City. The POA was allowed to intervene.

Arbitrator Paula Ann Hughes is associate dean at the University of Dallas, and it was up to her to decide exactly what control the City had over the bulletin board in police headquarters. The contract required the City to provide a bulletin board for the POA, but there was no prohibition against other bulletin boards. She decided that the chief was within his rights in offering a board to the Fraternal Order. The contract did provide that the City was prohibited from assisting or financing any employee organization other than the POA, but, according to the arbitrator, allowing the Fraternal Order to use the bulletin board did not violate that provision.

The arbitrator also decided that the City could subsequently deny such use. "Management does have the right to change its mind and decide that no bulletin boards should exist, except as called for in the contract." She also ruled that the City had not interfered or restrained the exercise of employee rights as defined in the agreement. The grievances were denied.

Police unions are formed to serve their members and themselves, but sometimes they become wedded to the status quo and resist attempts by the department to make changes. The next few cases involve those kinds of situations, where a union is contesting attempts by a department to install a new procedure. Whether change is based on new technology or on an attempt by the department to modernize procedures, the union may argue that it should be subjected to collective bargaining.

Management's capacity to make changes is diminished if, every time the city wants to install new technology, it must indulge in bargaining. Change can be glacial. This tendency toward impasse is an aspect of police labor relations that adds to the frustrations of all concerned, and many people who have studied police organizations think that they need restructuring.

A MATTER OF WORKING CONDITIONS

Many police officers must work in old, poorly maintained buildings. The city may own the facility but cannot afford to maintain it, and the police department merely occupies the building. A case like this arose in Holyoke, Massachusetts on October 9, 1990. The arbitrator, Dr. Allan S. McCausland, formerly a professor of economics, now head of his own consulting firm, had to decide whether or not the City had made a good faith effort to correct the safety problems in the police headquarters.

There was no doubt about the disreputable condition of the police station or its continuing deterioration. The superintendent of public works testified that problems had existed from the time the building was constructed and that the City had spent $65,000 trying to repair the building even before it opened in 1980. Water leakage was rampant. The building had been built with a parking lot on the roof, and the weight of parked automobiles had caused extensive leaking.

The arbitrator inspected the building October 9, 1990, which happened to be a drizzly day. His inspection confirmed the prior testimony.

- There were buckets in the hallways and rooms throughout the building, collecting water from leaks. Plastic was hung over windows and wiring to direct the water into buckets.

- The ceilings and walls were soaked throughout the building. Parts had been torn out in an attempt to catch the water and allow for drying.

- Water dripped around many light fixtures and wall sockets, especially where walls and ceilings had not been torn out. Puddles were a common sight throughout the building in rooms and hallways.

- Carpeting originally glued to the floor had been torn up in an attempt to allow drying and to reduce the stench and mold. Areas where carpeting had not been removed were subject to mold.

- One office was closed off due to the stench caused by a combination of water leaks and inadequate ventilation. Mold was coming through new tiles in the crime prevention room, and tiles in the exercise room were rising off the floor.

- Air quality throughout the building was poor at best, and it was not uncommon to hear officers coughing.

The hearing that day took place in the community room. This room was not one of the worst but, typically, there were puddles on the floor. The rugs had been torn up, and portions of the ceiling had been ripped out, leaving wiring and the outside structure exposed. Plastic was draped around the walls and windows in an attempt to catch and funnel water into buckets. The room had a bad odor, and the air irritated the nose and throat.

The City argued that the police chief had tried to correct the safety problems in the building, and it presented evidence about the City's weak financial condition. The City had attempted to persuade the voters to authorize additional revenue. An auditor testified to the City's financial plight and a reduction in state funding.

But Dr. McCausland decided that the City had not made a good faith effort to resolve the problems, which had been in existence since 1980, some ten years before. The continuing deterioration of the police building showed that the City had not made a sufficient effort.

The recommendations made in a report issued by the state in 1989, for example, had not been carried out. The ventilation system had not been improved, and the water damage had not been fixed. Holding the arbitration hearing in the building where McCausland could see and smell the deterioration may have made a powerful impact on him. On November 7, 1990 he ordered the City to carry out the recommendations in the 1989 report but refused to retain jurisdiction to oversee compliance as the union requested.

The grievance had been filed under the collective bargaining contract between the International Brotherhood of Police Officers and the City. The contract required the employer to maintain safe working conditions.

This case is not intended to indicate that most police officers work in unsafe, deteriorating quarters, although some do. It does show that when the police department has to rely on other branches of the City to maintain police stations, the quality of maintenance may suffer. If working conditions deteriorate, the individual cop may work under additional pressure.

ARBITRATING OVER THE USE OF TELEVISION SETS

Sometimes grievances between police officers and the department seem trivial. For example, the police department in New Bedford, Massachusetts decided to ban television sets from desk areas on the theory that the image of police officers watching TV while on duty was prejudicial to the department's reputation.

For many years, police officers on desk duty at the City's three police stations had access to television sets, and in all three stations, the TV was within view of the desk officer. In one location, the set could not be seen by the public, but two of these televisions were visible. Also, the commanding officers in two of the three police stations had television sets in their offices.

When the desk officer was not busy, he would turn on the set, with the volume kept low. If a member of the public came into the station, the television was turned off or the volume turned down. Television sets were not operated during day shifts except on weekends for sports programs. During the night shift, when the station was not busy, the desk officer could watch TV. The TVs in the commanding officers' rooms were used at the discretion of the commanding officer.

The sets had been loaned or donated to the station by the police officers and the officers, as a group, paid for any repairs. The City paid nothing, either for the purchase or the upkeep of the sets. The City did provide TVs in the officers' break area. These were bought and maintained by the City, and they were provided for the use of police officers who were on lunch or coffee breaks.

In response to the ban on TV, the police union filed for arbitration. The union argued that the City had taken away a job benefit that was covered by the "maintenance of benefits" clause in the contract. The City should have bargained over the issue before making the change.

The City pointed out that there were still television sets that police officers could use on breaks. The chief's ban was limited to the use of TV sets in the work areas, because the City felt that those TVs prejudiced the public perception of police officers.

Arbitrator James S. Cooper explained that the issue was whether or not watching TV was an employee benefit. In previous cases involving firefighters, the use of a television set had been considered a mandatory subject of bargaining. The use of TV while on-duty was not regarded as part of the "core of entrepreneurial control." Cooper viewed this case as similar. The benefit had to be bargained over before it could be removed. He upheld the grievance. On the other hand, he pointed out that the police department has the right to regulate the use of the television sets so as to minimize any loss in efficiency or the safety of prisoners being held in the lock-up.

Of all the arbitration cases described in this book, it is difficult to think of a more trivial issue. Was this an abuse of the arbitration process? Why was there a need to submit such a modest disagreement to an impartial decision maker? Are desk officers so addicted to night time television that it raises epic bargaining concerns? In fact, collective bargaining can involve virtually any aspect of the working relationship, not just wages and fringe benefits.

CAN A POLICE DEPARTMENT INSTALL TICKET QUOTAS?

How many parking tickets must an officer issue? Quotas can become controversial when tickets are a source of revenue for the City, but they are part of the working conditions of the police. Such changes in working conditions must be bargained over before they are instituted, but some police departments prefer to install changes first, then defend against grievances later, which can be like pouring kerosene on a hot stove.

In Canton, Ohio the police department discovered, as a result of an outside audit, that patrol officers averaged less than three traffic arrests per month, a low level of traffic enforcement by the City's eighty-two patrol officers. To encourage patrolmen to enforce the traffic laws, the City installed a new system where each patrol officer was expected to meet a minimum number of points over a four week period. The points could be earned for various traffic citations: drunk driving was six points, moving violations, two points, and parking violations, one-half a point.

During the summer of 1988, the department initiated monthly evalua-tions of patrol officers, covering their work, safety record, absenteeism, and tardiness, and an officer who did not meet the minimum point quota would receive a letter from a supervisor that performance was unsatisfactory. According to the City, such a letter did not constitute disciplinary action. The monthly reports were not part of the officer's file; nevertheless, they could be used in a six month evaluation, which an officer could only contest through the grievance procedure.

The union claimed that the new system changed the nature of the patrol officer's job and increased the stress. The City should have negotiated the change, because Article 12 of the contract provided that, "All matters pertaining to wages, hours and other conditions of employment and the continuation, modification or deletion of an existing provision of a collective bargaining agreement are subject to collective bargaining." This language came from the state law on public employee bargaining.

A grievance was filed in September, 1988 and went to arbitration. The arbitrator, Hyman Cohen, said that although the City was not required to bargain on subjects reserved to management, there was an obligation to bargain where such changes would affect terms and conditions of employment, and the new system changed the way officers performed their job.

The City pointed out that only a few officers would be affected, because fewer than three officers had failed to meet the quota. Unfortunately for the City's position, one of the witnesses at the hearing was the president of the local union who had been given a warning letter.

To the surprise of the union, arbitrator Cohen decided that the City did have the right to institute the policy. He said that the change had a minimal impact on a patrol officer's work, and he drew a line between matters relating to "wages, hours and other conditions of employment," and management rights that were reserved to the City. The increase in law enforcement efficiency achieved by the new system outweighed its impact on patrol officers. He held that the City did not violate the agreement by unilaterally installing the change.

In collective bargaining, the parties are often engaged in such controversies, because virtually any change in methods of operation can be said to have changed working conditions. Usually, such disagreements are settled informally, but sometimes an arbitrator must be brought in to resolve the issue.

COMPUTERIZATION AS A BARGAINING ISSUE

As police departments computerize their statistics, performance becomes easier to measure. Police officers sometimes resist such efforts as an attempt to apply pressure, and their union may claim that the department should have submitted the change to collective bargaining. One such case arose in Andover, Massachusetts, where the police department had always compiled statistics and had required officers to record their activities, which were classified according to the action taken and the violation involved. Each kind of activity was given a code number.

In 1989, the department installed new software that produced charts showing the activity of each officer on each shift, which provided visual comparisons of one officer to another, and, for the first time, these charts were given to shift commanders. Some officers testified that they were shown the graphs and warned that their statistics were low. At least one officer was ordered to make more vehicle arrests. The police union, a local council of AFSCME, filed a grievance on June 25, 1990.

The Town said that the statistics were being used as they had always been, to make decisions on deployment and staffing and that this kind of information had been available for many years. The department had always used statistics, although there were no fixed standards of productivity or performance. This was covered by the broad management rights clause in the contract.

The union argued that by making such statistics available to shift officers, the Town had created a performance appraisal system in violation of its obligations under the collective bargaining agreement.

Arbitrator Garry J. Wooters did not agree with the union's position, because the contract did not prohibit productivity standards. Based on testimony about the bargaining history, he concluded that such standards were never prohibited by the contract, nor was he convinced that the charts created any new standard of productivity. The arbitrator also found nothing in the contract that would preclude a supervisor from speaking with a police officer about productivity. In any case, there was no evidence that new criteria were being used to punish officers for failing to meet minimum standards.

Even if the contract was interpreted to prohibit the establishment of productivity standards during its term, there was no sign of such a violation. There had been discussions of performance standards during prior bargaining sessions, but no restrictions on that subject were ever included in the contract.

The arbitrator carefully reviewed the language of the contract and heard testimony on the issues submitted. He found that sharing statistical information with shift commanders and individual officers did not constitute a new performance appraisal system.

Computerization facilitates the distribution of statistical information throughout all operating levels of an organization, and it would handicap management if that process were subjected to collective bargaining. Nevertheless, a police officer may see it differently, because a supervisor can then compare an individual's performance with that of other officers, and there may be more pressure on the officer to produce.

Inevitably, police departments are adopting modern management, sharing information, facilitating communications, and increasing employee participation. Individual police officers will be given more information about crime statistics and about their community. This will change the job and put more pressure on each officer to be productive.

A COMMUNITY CONFRONTATION LEADING TO EXCESSIVE FORCE

A case that highlights the need for police officers to be dispute resolvers was arbitrated in Oakland, California. It took place in the Acorn Housing Project, which is said to be a place where considerable drug traffic and shootings take place. At 1:00 PM on October 16, 1990, an experienced police officer with an excellent prior record had chased an armed suspect into the project. He called for backup but lost his man among the housing units.

The director of a recreation center located in the project heard several police cars arrive and came outside holding a pool stick. He saw one of the police cars backing into the project at excessive speed and yelled at the driver because of the children in the area. The police officer, returning from his chase, got into a shouting match with the director, which led to him ordering the man to put down his stick. The director refused. Then, the officer and his partner grabbed him, with the officer punching the director several times in the face, then in the stomach. Finally, he was thrown to the ground, handcuffed, and taken to jail.

An investigation of the incident by the department concluded that the officer had used excessive force, and the officer was suspended for thirty days by the chief of police. The Oakland Police Officers Association filed a grievance on the officer's behalf.

Because there were numerous witnesses, including the two other officers, the facts were not difficult to ascertain. The grievant had punched the center director in the face four times and four times in the stomach, while another officer held the man's hands behind his back. The Association based its defense of the grievant's actions on his excellent record, and the fact that the director was holding a weapon. Even if just cause existed for some punishment of the officer, it should be no more than a five day suspension.

Arbitrator William E. Riker pointed out that both of these men were worthy citizens. The grievant had been an outstanding police officer. The center director had not only contributed to the young in his troubled community, but he had worked closely with law enforcement officers to help educate youths to recognize that the police are not their enemy but are there to enable citizens to live a life free of fear. He had been a role model.

Thus, Riker said, this unfortunate incident could have been avoided, and he concluded that the grievant had used excessive force and should be punished. The grievant was correct in telling the director to drop the stick, because he had an obligation to take control of the situation, and the director should have followed his command. At this stage, however, the grievant violated the City's rules by using excessive force. There was no justification for striking the director, because this was not a matter of self-defense. There was no evidence that the director was aggressive.

The arbitrator's justification for allowing the thirty day suspension to stand was bolstered by the fact that the incident took place in an area that is constantly challenging civil authority. Many children had witnessed the beating of their recreation director. He pointed out that the incident "supports the rumors of the police brutality that responsible persons in law enforcement and the community have been diligently working to overcome." The grievance was denied.

SHOULD DANGEROUS JOBS BE HIGHLY PAID?

One final case is included in this chapter, and it relates to the rate of pay for members of a bomb squad. How much should officers be paid for risking their lives? How much would you have to be paid to cope with bombs?

In late 1969, the Minneapolis Police Department established a bomb squad that had two officers who were trained in disposing of explosive devices. Two additional officers were added in 1975. The bomb squad was on-call, round-the-clock, every day of the year and the squad's officers were required to wear a pager, to remain within thirty-five miles of the City, and to be available for duty if called. While on-call, they were prohibited from consuming alcohol.

In 1976, the sergeant of the bomb squad requested higher pay for his squad. During collective bargaining that year, the parties agreed to waive the requirement that those officers receive compensatory time for each hour on stand-by, but in exchange, they agreed that bomb squad members would be compensated with two hours' pay for every shift they were on-call. Members of the bomb squad earned over a thousand hours of extra compensatory time each year, and this continued until March of 1987.

In 1987 the deputy chief said that the bomb squad was no longer required to be on-call when they were not on regular duty. He cited economic justification for the discontinuance of the prior practice and said that some alternative form of compensation would be provided.

The union did not take action until it was clear that the stand-by pay would not be forthcoming, but on April 18, 1990 the union filed a grievance, asserting that the employer had violated that bargaining agreement. The union demanded retroactive pay.

The City asserted that it had the right to terminate the practice even though the contract gave the City the right to require bomb squad officers to provide on-call duty. In March of 1987, the City had revoked that practice for economic reasons.

Arbitrator James L. Reynolds had to decide whether or not the City had violated the collective bargaining contract when it unilaterally terminated the on-call practice. He listened to testimony as to past practice, and he studied the contract.

There was no disagreement as to the facts. The question was not whether the City had the right to require the officers to respond to calls during their off-duty hours. Rather, the issue was whether an established compensation practice, such as the practice of two hours of compensatory time, could be discontinued unilaterally. Did the employer violate the contract when it denied compensatory time to members of the bomb squad?

The employer took its chances by discontinuing this practice, because it took the risk that it would not have the ability to respond to a bomb incident. Since the employer accepted that responsibility, arbitrator Reynolds denied the grievance.

SUMMARY

The cases in this chapter relate to determining which issues are subject to collective bargaining. Mostly, they involve the interplay between management rights and the city's obligation to negotiate certain changes in advance. Usually, the arbitrators upheld the right of police departments to make changes in their operation, which follows the normal trend of decisions. Arbitrators recognize the need for management to operate their organization but are sensitive to the contractual rights of employees in the bargaining unit.

CHAPTER 11

Police and Dispute Resolution

The cases in this book show examples of police officers disputing with their employer over discipline, employee rights, and contract language. These cases were actually decided by arbitrators, but they are not typical of normal police employment relationships. Arbitrations are exceptional, and most police departments operate year after year without a single grievance going to arbitration. Most disagreements are settled through relatively amicable discussions.

Still, one can learn from exceptions. These cases are informative, but what was there about these disputes that made them so difficult to settle? The issues do not seem unusually complicated, thereby making compromise impossible. Conflicting personalities may have blocked normal negotiations, or political considerations may have been involved. Community pressures may have given a difficult spin to the situation, or some other unexplained problem may have inhibited the particular parties.

One must admit that many of the grievances in this book seem remarkably trivial. A one or two day suspension can hardly be identified as major jurisprudence. Some of the grievants seem to be the Bozos of their departments, shooting bullets into the floor, failing to file reports, and wandering off in a patrol car without permission. Why were their unions willing to arbitrate on their behalf? Sometimes this is a mystery, because the cost of arbitration greatly exceeds the importance of some of these disputes. There must have been more to the story than what appeared in the arbitrator's award.

Collective bargaining governs the relationship between employers and their employees, but it was not intended to control the operation of the organization, which is the task of management. Bargaining, grievance processing, and arbitration are ways of resolving disagreements. In order for management to create better methods of operation, they must sometimes work with the union toward a shared goal, and this often requires a format other than grievance arbitration.

The individual police officer's right to be represented by a union in arbitration is valuable, because grievance arbitration offers unique access to the impartial review of management actions. Having the right to present such employee claims to an impartial arbitrator provides an important safeguard: Without arbitration, the contractual rights of police officers would be far less secure.

Arbitration protects both sides. Arbitrators enforce the police union's bargain, but if a cop violates the working rules, an arbitrator will uphold management's right to discipline the officer. Arbitrators must enforce the entire contract to deserve the day-to-day loyalty of its officers, but it also must do more: It must communicate. Working committees, including rank and file police officers, have been established in some situations, and informal meetings within the various precincts or divisions prove useful in others. These kinds of participative efforts are not necessarily inconsistent with collective bargaining. There is no conflict between a cop's wish to achieve a higher salary and better working conditions with the help of a union and the desire to be a productive officer of the law.

In the operation of a police department it is quite normal for disputes to arise. Some of these involve issues covered by the agreement, and these can be resolved through negotiations or arbitration, but others will involve operating policy questions. Then other methods to reconcile differences may be appropriate, and certain issues can be debated and resolved with the involvement of other people in the community.

It is not necessary for the police to rely entirely on collective bargaining. Many of the cases in this book could have been settled, but the union and the department may have adopted such entrenched positions that they were unable to compromise. It might have been useful for these parties to have used a trained mediator to facilitate a solution. A mediator does not make decisions for parties, as does an arbitrator, but helps them to analyze their problem to discover some way to agree on a mutually beneficial resolution.

Mediation is used to resolve many kinds of disputes, not only employee grievances. Some police departments use mediation to resolve community

disputes. The relationships between police and their community are intimate and complex, and controversies arise in many ways. Resolving them
can be unpleasant, and litigation is disruptive. Therefore, police officers
should be trained in mediation skills. Mediation is a sensible way to
encourage settlements. A mediator can work alone or as part of a team,
and one member of the team may be a police officer.

Professor Maria R. Volpe of John Jay Community College in New York,
a national authority on the police, believes that mediation has provided
better solutions when used by police officers. In her chapter, "Police Role,"
she explains:

> The potential of mediation for the police has yet to be fully tapped.
> While they are not in a position to conduct mediation under ideal
> conditions, mediation skills will enhance police officers' ability to
> listen carefully, communicate clearly and effectively with all parties
> as well as with partners, organize ideas logically in order to direct the
> flow of questioning, reason clearly and make sound judgments, and
> be alert to the implications of any action taken or questions asked.
> Mediation skills will also improve their ability to consider alternative
> courses of action, display resourcefulness and imagination, and es-
> tablish satisfactory relationships with others by being self-confident,
> knowledgeable, amenable, decisive, but flexible. Furthermore, me-
> diators know how to clarify underlying facts while keeping argu-
> ments and emotions within acceptable limits and help the parties to
> save face and lay the groundwork for improved communication in
> the future.
>
> The effective use of these skills and techniques enable police to
> defuse potentially difficult situations and demonstrate sensitivity and
> understanding toward disputants. By facilitating communication be-
> tween the parties, especially where they have a continuing relation-
> ship, agreements may be reached without official legal action,
> thereby saving police from processing the cases and testifying in
> court. (p. 232)

The nature of police work invites the greater use of mediation by police
officers, because many of the problems experienced by the police are
similar to those confronted by mediators in other settings; however,
mediation may not work when there are major disparities between the
parties. Mediation is a voluntary process, which works best when parties
are not being forced into the process.

SUMMARY

Police officers are authorized to use coercive force and must make relatively quick decisions, and although mediation can be used as a short-term intervention process, when used in the context of police work it may seem too time-consuming. Mediators must establish a negotiating climate and deal with substantive matters. Police traditionally prefer swift interventions rather than mediation. Furthermore, traditional police work has not been oriented toward consensual processes. When police productivity is measured by the number of summonses issued or arrests effected, mediated solutions are not rewarded.

But there are advantages to a process that involves people in their own resolution. Mediation tends to reduce conflict, to improve the social climate in a neighborhood, and to encourage people to verbalize their disagreements. It should be an important ingredient in community police work. Participating as a neutral in the resolution of such disputes can be a rewarding experience, and dealing with conflict offers a positive opportunity to help a community.

Cooperative working relationships between police officers and the people they serve would encourage both sides to maintain a peaceful environment, and this can augment the working life of the police officer.

The cases described in this book might not have arisen in a more consensual atmosphere. Unfortunately, relationships easily become adversarial. The grievants here were police officers, and their union and their employer were antagonists.

Arbitration resolves the stubborn grievances that cannot be settled through bilateral negotiations, but it should not be an arena for generating further hostility between the parties, and it should not be used too often. It is better for parties to resolve grievances amicably, relying on the earlier steps of the grievance procedures, working cooperatively to eliminate misunderstandings.

Conclusion

Some police officers will always work in a dangerous, stressful environment, where they are expected to respond to emergency situations of many kinds, and where handguns and other lethal firearms are a part of their environment. Cops are not always welcome in certain neighborhoods, because they may be a threat to some of the profitable illegal activities that are carried out there, or, as in some communities, they have come to be seen as an organization that is hostile to neighborhood youth and to the neighborhood itself.

Most urban police officers wear bulletproof vests, an indication of their anxiety. When police officers patrol hostile neighborhoods, there is always a concern for safety, and the scene is a dominant factor. Drug dealers operate in the open, often under the eyes of local residents, and they spread insecurity and fear. Drug dealers have taken over in some neighborhoods, and only when the police regain control can a secure environment be achieved. Residents should not have to endure the indignity of living in such environments.

The situation becomes more volatile when firearms are freely available, especially when, as sometimes happens, the criminal element has more firepower than the police. For the police officer, the war against crime means putting on a flack jacket and breaking into crack houses. To the extent that this increases the likelihood that police officers will be shot or injured, their job becomes increasingly stressful.

The working life of police officers, particularly in communities concerned with illegal drugs and violence, has become increasingly stressful. Some of the cases in this book illustrate the hazards and frustration of the job.

When concentrating on crushing the drug business, the police sometimes alienate local residents who look to them for protection. It is easy to be pessimistic and to view the United States as a country at war with itself. The police can be seen as representing the interests of property, imposing the criminal law upon poor, uneducated, minority people, and alienating them and sending them to prison.

An opportunity exists for genuine change toward a more community oriented police function, and many police commissioners and superintendents encourage that approach. Such a shift would give police officers responsibility for particular neighborhoods, and it would require a change from their present approach. Community policing would require a new partnership with the people in the neighborhoods. New priorities would have to be accepted by police officials, and new human resource practices, better recruiting, training, and reward systems would have to be part of the police structure.

Law abiding communities are built on trust, not on suppression, so when neighborhood children see police officers as their enemy, they become alienated from the larger community. There is no doubt that some kids fear the night stick and the gun as they watch patrol cars rolling past their street. In these cases, who is being protected and who is being kept down?

In neighborhoods where illegal drugs are sold on the street, where many young men are employed by drug dealers and where many residents see cops as their enemy, the police have become an occupation army. Does it have to be that way?

Older people have a fond memory of the foot patrolman, patting the heads of neighborhood kids, nodding to the local merchants, and building respect for the law. Now, in many cities, cops patrol the streets in armed cars and run their eyes across dark doorways. Their suspects may be lurking anywhere, and they may be a part of a drug enterprise that society says is criminal and evil but which it continues to patronize. Drug money has given criminals the power to play on the avarice of powerful people and to whet the appetite of millions of users. For the cop, this creates paranoia. Who can be trusted? In a pinch, will the neighborhood support the drug dealer or the police officer?

Is it possible for police departments in large urban centers to switch their attention toward community service in the chaos of the drug war, rather than enforcing the drug laws?

The New York City Police Department (NYPD) is huge with operating costs in the billions of dollars even with sharp cutbacks in the City's budget, and payroll is its major expense. With over 27,000 officers in uniform, the NYPD represents a large part of the municipal budget, therefore. This creates a monstrous challenge to the police: millions of poor people, a high crime rate, a huge drug industry, and a hot spot in the war against crime must be taken care of on a tight budget. How likely is it that cities like New York, at a time of fading resources, can devote themselves to community policing?

Another question is whether or not community policing is compatible with the drug war. Can a police department commit itself to keeping the peace and solving people's problems or must it be a para-military force fighting criminal organizations? Implementing a less confrontational approach will require major changes. Police officials have to be persuaded that problem solving and dispute resolution are of primary importance, and cops have to be trained to mediate.

Most modern corporations encourage better communications between executives and employees, and innovative management techniques have been created to accomplish that goal. Shared information is an important resource.

Skills in mediation, acquired as part of police training, can help to resolve all kinds of disputes. Every police officer can learn to mediate and to help resolve disputes. There are many opportunities for police officers as problem solvers, and cops should learn how to adjust differences. If they learn such techniques, they will find many uses for them on the job.

But how can this be accomplished? Disagreements constantly arise in a police officer's work within a local community, and dispute resolution can be learned on the job. An important goal should be to strengthen exactly those working skills. Training police officers in dispute resolution would strengthen every aspect of police work.

The community police movement is already making itself felt, changing departmental attitudes toward the function of the police officer and toward the community. Community policing may be the wave of the future. If so, it will motivate cops to better understand their role in dispute resolution.

Appendix: Labor Arbitration Rules

1.   Agreement of Parties

The parties shall be deemed to have made these rules a part of their arbitration agreement whenever, in a collective bargaining agreement or submission, they have provided for arbitration by the American Arbitration Association (hereinafter the AAA) or under its rules. These rules and any amendment thereof shall apply in the form obtaining when the arbitration is initiated. The parties, by written agreement, may vary the procedures set forth in these rules.

2.   Name of Tribunal

Any tribunal constituted by the parties under these rules shall be called the Labor Arbitration Tribunal.

3.   Administrator

When parties agree to arbitrate under these rules and an arbitration is instituted thereunder, they thereby authorize the AAA to administer the arbitration. The authority and obligations of the administrator are as provided in the agreement of the parties and in these rules.

4.   Delegation of Duties

The duties of the AAA may be carried out through such representatives or committees as the AAA may direct.

5.   Panel of Labor Arbitrators

The AAA shall establish and maintain a Panel of Labor Arbitrators and shall appoint arbitrators therefrom as hereinafter provided.

6.   Office of Tribunal

The general office of the Labor Arbitration Tribunal is the headquarters of the AAA, which may, however, assign the administration of an arbitration to any of its regional offices.

7.   Initiation under an Arbitration Clause in a Collective Bargaining Agreement

Arbitration under an arbitration clause in a collective bargaining agreement under these rules may be initiated by either party in the following manner:

(a) by giving written notice to the other party of its intention to arbitrate (demand), which notice shall contain a statement setting forth the nature of the dispute and the remedy sought, and

(b) by filing at any regional office of the AAA three copies of the notice, together with a copy of the collective bargaining agreement or such parts thereof as relate to the dispute, including the arbitration provisions. After the arbitrator is appointed, no new or different claim may be submitted except with the consent of the arbitrator and all other parties.

8.   Answer

The party upon whom the demand for arbitration is made may file an answering statement with the AAA within ten days after notice from the AAA, simultaneously sending a copy to the other party. If no answer is filed within the stated time, it will be treated as a denial of the claim. Failure to file an answer shall not operate to delay the arbitration.

9.   Initiation under a Submission

Parties to any collective bargaining agreement may initiate an arbitration under these rules by filing at any regional office of the AAA two copies of a written agreement to arbitrate under these rules (submission), signed by the parties and setting forth the nature of the dispute and the remedy sought.

10.   Fixing of Locale

The parties may mutually agree on the locale where the arbitration is to be held. If the locale is not designated in the collective bargaining agreement or submission, and if there is a dispute as to the appropriate locale, the AAA shall have the power to determine the locale and its decision shall be binding.

11.   Qualifications of Arbitrator

Any neutral arbitrator appointed pursuant to Section 12, 13, or 14 or selected by mutual choice of the parties or their appointees, shall be subject to disqualification for the reasons specified in Section 17. If the parties specifically so agree in writing, the arbitrator shall not be subject to disqualification for those reasons.

Unless the parties agree otherwise, an arbitrator selected unilaterally by one party is a party-appointed arbitrator and is not subject to disqualification pursuant to Section 17.

The term "arbitrator" in these rules refers to the arbitration panel, whether composed of one or more arbitrators and whether the arbitrators are neutral or party appointed.

12.   Appointment from Panel

If the parties have not appointed an arbitrator and have not provided any other method of appointment, the arbitrator shall be appointed in the following manner: immediately after the filing of the demand or submission, the AAA shall submit simultaneously to each party an identical list of names of persons chosen from the Panel of Labor Arbitrators. Each party shall have ten days from the mailing date in which to strike any name to which it objects, number the remaining names to indicate the order of preference, and return the list to the AAA.

If a party does not return the list within the time specified, all persons named therein shall be deemed acceptable.

From among the persons who have been approved on both lists, and in accordance with the designated order of mutual preference, the AAA shall invite the acceptance of an arbitrator to serve. If the parties fail to agree upon any of the persons named, if those named decline or are unable to act, or if for any other reason the appointment cannot be made from the submitted lists, the administrator shall have the power to make the appointment from among other members of the panel without the submission of any additional list.

13.   Direct Appointment by Parties

If the agreement of the parties names an arbitrator or specifies a method of appointing an arbitrator, that designation or method shall be followed. The notice of appointment, with the name and address of the arbitrator, shall be filed with the AAA by the appointing party, Upon the request of any appointing party, the AAA shall submit a list of members of the panel from which the party may, if it so desires, make the appointment.

If the agreement specifies a period of time within which an arbitrator shall be appointed and any party fails to make an appointment within that period, the AAA may make the appointment.

If no period of time is specified in the agreement, the AAA shall notify the parties to make the appointment and if within ten days thereafter such arbitrator has not been so appointed, the AAA shall make the appointment.

14. Appointment of Neutral Arbitrator by Party-Appointed Arbitrators

If the parties have appointed their arbitrators or if either or both of them have been appointed as provided in Section 13, and have authorized those arbitrators to appoint a neutral arbitrator within a specified time and no appointment is made within that time or any agreed extension thereof, the AAA may appoint a neutral arbitrator who shall act as chairperson.

If no period of time is specified for appointment of the neutral arbitrator and the parties do not make the appointment within ten days from the date of the appointment of the last party-appointed arbitrator, the AAA shall appoint a neutral arbitrator who shall act as chairperson.

If the parties have agreed that the arbitrators shall appoint the neutral arbitrator from the panel, the AAA shall furnish to the party-appointed arbitrators, in the manner prescribed in Section 12, a list selected from the panel, and the appointment of the neutral arbitrator shall be made as prescribed in that section.

15. Number of Arbitrators

If the arbitration agreement does not specify the number of arbitrators, the dispute shall be heard and determined by one arbitrator, unless the parties otherwise agree.

16. Notice to Arbitrator of Appointment

Notice of the appointment of the neutral arbitrator shall be mailed to the arbitrator by the AAA and the signed acceptance of the arbitrator shall be filed with the AAA prior to the opening of the first hearing.

17. Disclosure and Challenge Procedure

No person shall serve as a neutral arbitrator in any arbitration under these rules in which that person has any financial or personal interest in the result of the arbitration. Any prospective or designated neutral arbitrator shall immediately disclose any circumstance likely to affect impartiality, including any bias or financial or personal interest in the result of the arbitration. Upon receipt of this information from the arbitrator or another source, the AAA shall communicate the information to the parties and, if it deems it appropriate to do so, to the arbitrator. Upon objection of a party to the continued service of a neutral arbitrator, the AAA, after consultation with the parties and the arbitrator, shall determine whether the arbitrator should be disqualified and shall inform the parties of its decision, which shall be conclusive.

18. Vacancies

If any arbitrator should resign, die, or otherwise be unable to perform the duties of the office, the AAA shall, on proof satisfactory to it, declare the office vacant. Vacancies shall be filled in the same manner as that governing the making of the original appointment, and the matter shall be reheard by the new arbitrator.

19. Date, Time, and Place of Hearing

The arbitrator shall fix the date, time, and place for each hearing. At least five days prior thereto, the AAA shall mail notice of the date, time, and place of hearing to each party, unless the parties otherwise agree.

20. Representation

Any party may be represented by counsel or other authorized representative.

21. Stenographic Record and Interpreters

Any party wishing a stenographic record shall make arrangements directly with a stenographer and shall notify the other parties of such arrangements in advance of the hearing. The requesting party or parties shall pay the cost of the record. If the transcript is agreed by the parties to be or, in appropriate cases, determined by the arbitrator to be the official record of the proceeding, it must be made available to the arbitrator and to the other party for inspection, at a time and place determined by the arbitrator.

Any party wishing an interpreter shall make all arrangements directly with the interpreter and shall assume the costs of the service.

22. Attendance at Hearings

Persons having a direct interest in the arbitration are entitled to attend hearings. The arbitrator shall have the power to require the retirement of any witness or witnesses during the testimony of other witnesses. It shall be discretionary with the arbitrator to determine the propriety of the attendance of any other person.

23.   Postponements

The arbitrator for good cause shown may postpone the hearing upon the request of a party or upon his or her own initiative and shall postpone when all of the parties agree thereto.

24.   Oaths

Before proceeding with the first hearing, each arbitrator may take an oath of office and, if required by law, shall do so. The arbitrator may require witnesses to testify under oath administered by any duly qualified person and, if required by law or requested by either party, shall do so.

25.   Majority Decision

Whenever there is more than one arbitrator, all decisions of the arbitrators shall be by majority vote. The award shall also be made by majority vote unless the concurrence of all is expressly required.

26.   Order of Proceedings

A hearing shall be opened by the filing of the oath of the arbitrator, where required; by the recording of the date, time, and place of the hearing and the presence of the arbitrator, the parties, and counsel, if any; and by the receipt by the arbitrator of the demand and answer, if any, or the submission.

Exhibits may, when offered by either party, be received in evidence by the arbitrator. The names and addresses of all witnesses and exhibits in order received shall be made a part of the record.

The arbitrator may vary the normal procedure under which the initiating party first presents its claim, but in any case shall afford full and equal opportunity to all parties for the presentation of relevant proofs.

27.   Arbitration in the Absence of a Party or Representative

Unless the law provides to the contrary, the arbitration may proceed in the absence of any party or representative who, after due notice, fails to be present or fails to obtain a postponement. An award shall not be made solely on the default of a party. The arbitrator shall require the other party to submit such evidence as may be required for the making of an award.

28.   Evidence

The parties may offer such evidence as is relevant and material to the dispute, and shall produce such additional evidence as the arbitrator may deem necessary to an understanding and determination of the dispute. An arbitrator authorized by law to subpoena witnesses and documents may do so independently or upon the request of any party. The arbitrator shall be the judge of the relevance and materiality of the evidence offered and conformity to legal rules of evidence shall not be necessary. All evidence shall be taken in the presence of all of the arbitrators and all of the parties except where any of the parties is absent in default or has waived the right to be present.

29. Evidence by Affidavit and Filing of Documents

The arbitrator may receive and consider the evidence of witnesses by affidavit, giving it only such weight as seems proper after consideration of any objection made to its admission.

All documents that are not filed with the arbitrator at the hearing, but arranged at the hearing or subsequently by agreement of the parties to be submitted, shall be filed with the AAA for transmission to the arbitrator. All parties shall be afforded opportunity to examine such documents.

30. Inspection

Whenever the arbitrator deems it necessary, he or she may make an inspection in connection with the subject matter of the dispute after written notice to the parties, who may, if they so desire, be present at the inspection.

31. Closing of Hearings

The arbitrator shall inquire of all parties whether they have any further proof to offer or witness to be heard. Upon receiving negative replies or if satisfied that the record is complete, the arbitrator shall declare the hearings closed and a minute thereof shall be recorded. If briefs or other documents are to be filed, the hearings shall be declared closed as of the final date set by the arbitrator for filing with the AAA. If documents are to be filed as provided in Section 29 and the date for their receipt is later than the date set for the receipt of briefs, the later date shall be the date of closing the hearing. The time limit within which the arbitrator is required to make an award shall commence to run, in the absence of another agreement by the parties, upon the closing of the hearings.

32. Reopening of Hearings

The hearings may for good cause shown be reopened by the arbitrator at will or on the motion of either party at any time before the award is made but, if the reopening of the hearings would prevent the making of the award within the specific time agreed upon by the parties in the contract out of which the controversy has arisen, the matter may not be reopened unless both parties agree to extend the time. When no specific date is fixed in the contract, the arbitrator may reopen the hearings and shall have thirty days from the closing of the reopened hearings within which to make an award.

33.   Waiver of Oral Hearings

The parties may provide, by written agreement, for the waiver of oral hearings. If the parties are unable to agree as to the procedure, the AAA shall specify a fair and equitable procedure.

34.   Waiver of Rules

Any party who proceeds with the arbitration after knowledge that any provision or requirement of these rules has not been complied with and who fails to state an objection thereto in writing shall be deemed to have waived the right to object.

35.   Extensions of Time

The parties may modify any period of time by mutual agreement. The AAA or the arbitrator may for good cause extend any period of time established by these rules, except the time for making the award. The AAA shall notify the parties of any such extension of time and its reason therefor.

36.   Serving of Notice

Each party to a submission or other agreement that provides for arbitration under these rules shall be deemed to have consented and shall consent that any papers, notices, or process necessary or proper for the initiation or continuation of an arbitration under these rules; for any court action in connection therewith; or for the entry of judgment on an award made thereunder may be served upon the party by mail addressed to the party or its representative at the last known address or by personal service, in or outside the state where the arbitration is to be held.

The AAA and the parties may also use facsimile transmission, telex, telegram, or other written forms of electronic communication to give the notices required by these rules.

37.   Time of Award

The award shall be rendered promptly by the arbitrator and, unless otherwise agreed by the parties or specified by law, no later than thirty days from the date of closing the hearings, with five additional days for mailing if briefs are to be filed.

If oral hearings have been waived, the award shall be rendered no later than thirty days from the date of transmitting the final statements and proofs to the arbitrator.

38.   Form of Award

The award shall be in writing and shall be signed either by the neutral arbitrator or by a concurring majority if there is more than one arbitrator.

The parties shall advise the AAA whenever they do not require the arbitrator to accompany the award with an opinion.

39.   Award upon Settlement

If the parties settle their dispute during the course of the arbitration, the arbitrator may, upon their request, set forth the terms of the agreed settlement in an award.

40.   Delivery of Award to Parties

Parties shall accept as legal delivery of the award the placing of the award or a true copy thereof in the mail by the AAA, addressed to the party at its last known address or to its representative; personal service of the award; or the filing of the award in any other manner that is permitted by law.

41.   Release of Documents for Judicial Proceedings

The AAA shall, upon the written request of a party, furnish to such party, at its expense, certified facsimiles of any papers in the AAA's possession that may be required in judicial proceedings relating to the arbitration.

42.   Judicial Proceedings and Exclusion of Liability

(a) Neither the AAA nor any arbitrator in a proceeding under these rules is a necessary party in judicial proceedings relating to the arbitration.

(b) Neither the AAA nor any arbitrator shall be liable to any party for any act or omission in connection with any arbitration conducted under these rules.

43.   Administrative Fees

As a not-for-profit organization, the AAA shall prescribe an administrative fee schedule to compensate it for the cost of providing administrative services. The schedule in effect at the time of filing shall be applicable.

44.   Expenses

The expenses of witnesses for either side shall be paid by the party producing such witnesses.

Expenses of the arbitration, other than the cost of the stenographic record, including required traveling and other expenses of the arbitrator and of AAA representatives and the expenses of any witness or the cost of any proof produced at the direct request of the arbitrator, shall be borne equally by the parties, unless they agree otherwise, or unless the arbitrator, in the award, assesses such expenses or any part thereof against any specified party or parties.

45. Communication with Arbitrator

There shall be no communication between the parties and a neutral arbitrator other than at oral hearings, unless the parties and the arbitrator agree otherwise. Any other oral or written communication from the parties to the arbitrator shall be directed to the AAA for transmittal to the arbitrator.

46. Interpretation and Application of Rules

The arbitrator shall interpret and apply these rules insofar as they relate to the arbitrator's powers and duties. When there is more than one arbitrator and a difference arises among them concerning the meaning or application of any such rule, it shall be decided by a majority vote. If that is unobtainable, the arbitrator or either party may refer the question to the AAA for final decision. All other rules shall be interpreted and applied by the AAA.

Administrative Fees

Initial Administrative Fee

The initial administrative fee is $125 for each party, due and payable at the time of filing. No refund of the initial fee is made when a matter is withdrawn or settled after the filing of the demand for arbitration or submission.

Arbitrator Compensation

Unless mutually agreed otherwise, the arbitrator's compensation shall be borne equally by the parties, in accordance with the fee structure disclosed in the arbitrator's biographical profile submitted to the parties.

Additional Hearing Fees

A fee of $50 is payable by each party for each hearing held after the first hearing.

Hearing Room Rental

Hearing rooms for second and subsequent hearings are available on a rental basis at AAA offices. Check with your local office for specific availability and rates.

Postponement Fees

A fee of $50 is payable by a party causing a postponement of any scheduled hearing.

Bibliography

BOOKS AND ARTICLES

Coulson, Robert. *Labor Arbitration—What You Need to Know*. Rev. 3rd ed. New York: American Arbitration Association, 1988.

Deitsch, Clarence R., and David D. Dilts. *The Arbitration of Rights Disputes in the Public Sector*. Westport, Conn.: Quorum Books, 1990.

Delaney, John Thomas, Peter Feuille, and Wallace Hendricks. "Interest Arbitration and Grievance Arbitration: The Twain Do Meet." In Industrial Relations Research Association, *Proceedings of the Thirty-Sixth Annual Meeting, December 28-30, 1983, San Francisco*, pp. 313–320. Madison, WI: Industrial Relations Research Association, 1984.

Elkouri, Frank, and Edna Asper Elkouri. *How Arbitration Works*. 4th ed. Washington, DC: Bureau of National Affairs, 1985.

LaVan, Helen, and Cameron Carley. "Analysis of Arbitrated Employee Grievance Cases in Police Departments." *Journal of Collective Negotiations in the Public Sector*, vol. 14, no. 3 (1985), pp. 245–254.

Marmo, Michael. "Off-Duty Behavior by Police: Arbitrators Determine If On-the-Job Discipline Is Appropriate." *Journal of Police Science and Administration*, vol. 14, no. 2 (1986), pp. 102–111.

Silver, Isidore. *Public Employee Discharge and Discipline*. New York: John Wiley, 1989. Includes 1992 cumulative supplement through February 1, 1992.

Volpe, Maria. "Police Role." In *Mediations and Criminal Justice: Victims, Offenders, and Community*, edited by Martin White and Burt Galloway. London: Sage Publications, 1989.

Zack, Arnold. *Understanding Grievance Arbitration in the Public Sector*. Washington, DC: U.S. Department of Labor, Labor-Management Services Administration, 1980.

NEWSLETTERS AND REPORTING SERVICES

Arrest Law Bulletin. Boston: Quinlan.

Government Employee Relations Report. Washington, DC: Bureau of National Affairs.

Labor Arbitration Awards. Chicago: Commerce Clearing House.

Labor Arbitration in Government. New York: American Arbitration Association.

Labor Arbitration Information System. Horsham, PA: LRP Press.

Labor Arbitration Reports. Washington, DC: Bureau of National Affairs.

Police Officer Grievances Bulletin. Boston: Quinlan.

Index of Cases

CHAPTER 5

CHAPTER 6

CHAPTER 7

CHAPTER 8

Index

About the Author

ROBERT COULSON has been the President of the American Arbitration Association since 1972 and has written extensively about the settlement of disputes. He is a member of the American Bar Association, former chair of its Commercial Arbitration Committee, with a LLB degree from Harvard Law School. His books include *Labor Arbitration* (1986), *Business Arbitration* (1986), *How to Stay Out of Court* (1984), *Fighting Fair* (1983), and *Empowered at Forty* (1990), among others.